THE ABSURDITY CORRECTNESS & RACISM

Liam Wolford

Copyright © 2009 by Liam Wolford

http://www.politicallyabsurd.com

First Addition

CONTENTS

INTRODUCTION 6

Chapter 1 — What is a Racist 9

Chapter 2 — Extremes 21

Chapter 3 — Deportation 23

Chapter 4 — Extremities vs. Balance 34

Chapter 5 — Blonde Haired, Blue Eyed Extinction 41

Chapter 6 — Lebensborn 44

Chapter 7 — Iceland 46

Chapter 8 — 100 Years of Destruction 48

Chapter 9 — The Blame Game 51

Chapter 10 — Population Control 57

Chapter 11 — Welfare 60

Chapter 12 — Crime 62

Chapter 13 — Happiness 68

Chapter 14 — Morals 73

Chapter 15 — Immigration 78

Chapter 16 — Greed 84

Chapter 17 — Obvious Problems 88

Chapter 18 — War 92

Chapter 19   *Transportation 94*

Chapter 20   *Hostile Liberals 97*

Chapter 21   *Germans and Their Nazi Past 105*

New Policies 116

"I have a dream that little children will one day live in a nation where they will not be judged by the color of their skin but by the content of their character."

- Dr. Martin Luther King Jr.

INTRODUCTION

This a comprehensive book about serious racial, social, economic, environmental and political issues. One of the main themes is reverse prejudice and the absurdity of political correctness. Political correctness was designed to prevent discrimination, oppression and abuse. However, it is getting so far out of hand that it is endangering the very existence of the U.S. and other first world nations. Consistently racism is associated with whites; in large part, because of the history of whites and how they treated other races. The most notable examples would be the systematic killing of millions of Jews by the Nazis and the African slave trade.

However, racism has taken on a new face in recent decades and this book goes beyond political correctness and looks at the world and the people in it honestly and without the veil of political correctness that hides that truth. An example is how much of Europe, the US and other first world nations are being overrun by immigrants who refuse to assimilate and detest the indigenous population, their language, culture, customs and religions, yet some reap and take advantage of our tolerance, freedoms and social benefits.

Are the citizens who object to this unarmed invasion really racist as they are accused, or are their concerns legitimate? Are we ignoring the obvious dangers for the sake of being politically correct?

This is an honest and radical topic that most tread lightly upon or ignore and avoid altogether for fear of repercussions. Both those in agreement and disagreement will find something in this book that reflects their point of view. Although, this book is objective and tolerant towards everyone, things will be said that most are afraid to say even though they know in their hearts that it is true, because of the fear of being labeled a racist in a time of black U. S. Presidents and extreme political correctness.

This is also a book about political and social ideology. There are many political systems that seemed to have the answers to the world's problems, yet for one reason or another they have failed, I.e. Communism, fascism, totalitarianism, socialism and even a democratic, free enterprise system has its flaws! However, none of these political systems would have taken roots if there was not something desirable about them.

For example; Communism is about equality! Whether you're an uneducated drunk or a doctor, you get the same paycheck, because everyone is treated as an equal. The good in all of this is that there are no homeless and this system creates strong family and social bonds; the bad is that the hard working entrepreneurs, doctors, scientist, etc. are not rewarded for their efforts, thus creating a society without the drive to succeed and create!

In this book I will present ideas for balance and how the good ideas can be implemented in a political system without crippling individual efforts and the entrepreneur spirit of the free enterprise system!

One thing that I want to make clear from the beginning of this book is that I do not support any group that in anyway promotes and encourage hate, prejudice and racism towards others. I believe that everyone has a right to exist and to be treated with kindness, respect, fairness, equality and dignity by all other groups regardless of race, religion, sexual preference, gender, age or disability, etc! Many of my opinions may be viewed as racist by some in this hyper-sensitive PC society we live, and in all honesty if you read the Webster's definition of racism I suppose I could fall into that category?

The definition of a racist according to Webster's is **"A belief that race is the primary determinant of human traits and capacities and those racial differences produce an inherent superiority of a particular race"**

So, maybe I am racist according to Webster's dictionary in some ways? However, I still don't see myself as a racist despite what the definition may say?

When I think of a racist I think of someone who has a total intolerance for another group and I don't see myself that way at all! What this all comes down to is an opinion and a desire for a world that is safer, cleaner, more tolerant and sustainable, a world where you would want to raise your children, a clean safe beautiful world and yes, a world that sees the value of preserving different cultures and races.

This is a book about my opinions, as well as extensive research, and although my personal opinions will undoubtedly differ greatly from how some others may see the world, I will present honest data and thought provoking ideas, all of which focus on the greater good of society and will create an honest and healthy debate regarding some very serious issues!

I think one of the biggest misconceptions and controversies associated with this book will be that the ideology might resemble in some ways socialism or some may even say that many of my ideas more closely resemble a fascist ideology? Whenever words like race, Aryan, blonde hair and blue-eyes are used it is easy to head strait to that conclusion. However, I do not necessarily believe that any one trait has an advantage over another. I do however believe in the preservation of certain traits. In fact I believe in the preservation of all traits and of all races. I might focus in on specific traits and races just because of the fact that they are endangered, but not necessarily because I feel that in any way that they are superior.

It is evident that some cultures have a better way of thinking and managing, but not necessarily because of the ethnicity of those cultures. There are many other factors to be considered. For example something like inventiveness might simply come from necessity and not lack of ability. When the Europeans began settling the west the native inhabitants had not even invented the wheel yet. Some might think it is because they are intellectually inferior, but perhaps they just didn't need it?

A lot of our greatest inventions come from wars, because of the need to survive and win the war, but if there were no wars would many of these Inventions have been realized? The Native Americans survived for thousands of years without the inventions the Europeans had simply because there was really no need for them.

Chapter 1

What is a Racist?

Maybe I am a racist, but not prejudice? Prejudice is a preconceived judgment or opinion, an adverse opinion or leaning formed without just grounds or before sufficient knowledge, an instance of such judgment or opinion, an irrational attitude of hostility directed against an individual, a group, a race, or their supposed characteristics.

I see part of my opinions in both definitions, but certainly not all! I don't believe that I have an irrational hostility towards groups or individuals. I also don't believe that I have preconceived judgments without grounds. There is plenty of evidence and grounds for my opinions.

Clearly we are kidding ourselves if we can't admit that there are distinct differences between races and cultures, and I am not talking about the obvious superficial characteristics, but more about the attitudes and the overall way of thinking that certain groups have! However, because of political correctness we deny or ignore what we see? Many of the differences could have to do with environment more than race? But, in some cases people create their environment. This is a choice and an attitude. I do however see bad choices and attitudes in all races and cultures, which can't be blamed entirely on environment.

Some impoverished cultures are violent, while other impoverished cultures with just as little or less are happy, friendly, loving and non-violent. Why is this? I think that there are many factors including environment, religious beliefs, past circumstances and genetics. Genetics could fall into the race category. Although, all humans are so genetically similar, can you really say that any one race is better than another? I do however feel that the small genetic and or cultural differences can result in significant differences in lifestyle and attitudes!

However, these are merely my opinions and are not designed to harm anyone, with the exception of my views on criminal punishment. Those who harm innocent people are a separate category. I don't agree with the extremist who wants to wipe certain races and cultures from the earth. I don't believe in hating or harming individuals because they are of a different ethnic, religious or social group. However, one of my strongest opinions is that innocent people should be protected!

I admittedly have NO understanding of why someone would want to hurt an innocent person or child? The key word is innocent, because I have NO remorse when it comes to the punishment of those who do harm to the innocent victims of the world. From the local school bully to the child molesters all the way to the radical extremists who have no qualms about obtaining and using weapons of mass destruction on innocent victims!

I mention particular ethnic groups, not because of their race, but because of their actions. This will be labeled racism, but it is reality and there are statistics to prove it. This certainly does not mean that people should generalize races, cultures or religions. Individuals should be seen as independent, because we all have the freedom of choice!

There are other groups where it may seem as if I have a preference? This will also be labeled racism. Martin Luther King Jr. Said it best: "Let a man be judged on his character and not the color of his skin" I believe in this statement whole-heartedly! So, when you see a group of black teenagers harassing, intimidating, cussing, shooting, raping and robbing people they should be judged on their character. The same applies for any other ethnic group of teenagers engaging in similar activities. The fact that I used black teenagers as my example would also lead people to believe that I am a racist, but the choice of example comes from statistics and not an irrational leaning towards a particular group. I could have been politically correct and glanced over these statistics, but I am honest and the statistics speak for themselves; they are what they are, like it or not.

Merely reading the introduction to this book will no doubt cause controversy and anger from many! In an age that is constantly reminded of the horrors of the holocaust and the slave trade, we have become hyper sensitive to any real or perceived injustices towards ethnic or religious groups. An example of a perceived injustice might be in the case of a Caucasian winning a job over a minority or vice versa, when in reality the decision may have been based on ability, experience or both as it should be! However, some will insist that racism, prejudice or reverse prejudice played a role. And it is this absurdity and relentless pressure that forces many employers to hire a less qualified person as to not offend anyone or to be labeled with some sort of undesirable and politically incorrect title.

I get the impression that many Germans almost feel guilty and ashamed for being German because of this sort of pressure and their Nations Nazi past. However, the Germans are not unique. The United States and many European countries are also reminded of their past iniquities in their treatment of other races and rightfully so! The horrors are inexcusable and we should be reminded of the past, so it never repeats itself! However, because of the extremes of the past attitudes and treatment of many races, the white race has almost condemned itself to extinction.

The white Americans and especially the Germans seem to go to great lengths to erase and forget the past. Many white Americans are very careful and even fearful of stepping on anybody's toes! The term African American is just the latest attempt to show respect to the black race because of the sins of our forefathers.

I feel that a great deal of preference is paid to other races because of the sins of some of our forefathers! As an American with English, German and Scandinavian ancestry I often wonder why I am not addressed as a European American. Wouldn't that be fair and equal treatment? I am described as white. Why do blacks need this special distinction? We are basically kissing ass for something we did not do! One thing that blacks need to remember is that the majority of white soldiers in the Civil War fought and died to free them and never agreed with the slave trade!

The American Civil War from 1861 to 1865 was a war to abolish slavery and to prevent the secession of the Southern States from the Union. The South mainly wanted to secede for economic reasons, mainly cotton, which in effect was so lucrative, because of slavery. Therefore, the main reason for the Civil War goes back to the use of slaves. There were 11 Southern States who were pro slavery and 25 Northern or Union states that were against slavery. Before President Lincolns Administration took office March 4th 1861, seven Southern States declared secession and joined to form the Confederate States of America; another 8 slave states rejected the secession at this time.

James Buchanan the president before Abraham Lincoln took office rejected the legality of secession and hostilities broke out on April 12th, 1861 when the South fired on Fort Sumter in South Carolina.

The American Civil War became the deadliest war in United States history with the deaths of 625,000 soldiers and an undetermined number of civilians; exceeding World War 1, World War 2, The Korean War and the Vietnam War combined!

10% of all Northern males between the ages of 20-45 died as a result of the American Civil War, all in the name of preventing secession, abolishing slavery, and freeing blacks from what was seen as an anachronistic evil by MOST whites. So, even during one of the most racist periods in our history, thousands of white soldiers willingly fought and died (whites killing whites) to free the African slaves. However, some African Americans seem to overlook this fact and view whites in general as racist, when in reality there were only a minority of whites who were really racist.

The white race WAS, responsible for the abolition of slavery and not the blacks. It was not a black revolt or protest that started the Civil War which ended slavery; it was the whites who ended slavery. Although, blacks undoubtedly had a contributing factor and fought alongside white Union soldiers; at the time, they had no rights or the power to make any political or social changes. Yet, all whites are lumped into the same racist category. To a lot of blacks there are NO distinctions, just lump them all into one category; RACIST!

As controversial as this topic is, I really felt that someone needed to open up and say something about how ridiculous this has all become! The race card is favorite one to play by many non-white races and reverse prejudice has become the new prejudice. The noose seems to be getting tighter and tighter for the white race, because we are allowing it.

It has come to a point where it is not balanced and fair, but absurd! Other races I am sure feel that this is entirely justifiable considering the past transgressions of the white race. I stress the point "Past Transgressions" because, the people of those times are ghosts and those ideas no longer exist (for the most part) and the present people should not be condemned for the actions of those in the past! It is like condemning every German because there were Nazis! Which, by the way is something that the victorious nations tried to do after World War 2.

There is no doubt that when the white Europeans came to the New World they committed horrible crimes against the indigenous population and the environment. It started with Christopher Columbus. At first the natives befriended the new comers only to be taken advantage of later on. The explorers raped, murdered and enslaved their hosts and treated them as sub-human, while at the same time exploiting the land. When the Indians retaliated they were labeled as savages and thousands were murdered as a result. In the years to come the Indians would be murdered, enslaved, raped and stripped of their land. The white man would make and break treaties with the Indians for the benefit of only the white man.

One of the more notable treaty violations was the 1868 Treaty of Fort Laramie. This treaty confirmed the Lakota Indians ownership of the Black Hills mountain range. Native Americans had occupied this Sacred land since 7000 BC. However, when gold was discovered in the 1870's the United States took control from the Lakota in violation of the Treaty of Fort Laramie simply out of greed.

The wasteful slaughter of the bison is another example of how far the white man would go to take control of Indian land. By killing off the bison the whites depleted the Indians food supply and took the valuable hides that the Indians used to make shelter and clothing. The Indians used every part of the bison, where the white man just took the hide, then left the rotting carcasses to waste away. At the beginning of the 19th century there were nearly 75 million bison, but by the beginning of the 20th century there were only 540 roaming freely. The white man hunted the bison mercilessly, rendering them nearly extinct! Now tell me who were the real savages? Believe me I fully understand how bad the white man was and in some cases still is!

The remains of the once proud buffalo which ruled the plains

Despite the religious and moral convictions of our founding fathers, they seemed to feel perfectly entitled to go to Africa and pick up slaves to do their work. Since blacks were viewed as sub-human and inferior by whites, I guess they felt that the religious morals and convictions that applied to whites did not apply to blacks?

The exploitation of natural resources is another grievance of mine. Strip mining, de-forestation, and the extinction of much of our wildlife are particularly hard to swallow! Believe me I certainly understand grievances with the early white settlers! But, we are, where we are now, and we need to stop looking at the past and looking towards the future. It is unrealistic that the white people will go back to Europe, the blacks will go back to Africa, the Asians will go back to Asia or the Mexicans will go back to Mexico. Especially since some people have a piece of every one of those ethnic groups in them.

However, we do need to put those things behind us and try to preserve what is left of our environment and of our individual ethnic groups!

My Fiancée was born and raised in Hungary and recently she took me to a Hungarian Christmas party, where I enjoyed traditional Hungarian music, dance and food! Many of the children who participated were born in the US and some had probably never even been to Hungary. Yet, they were taught the traditions and language of their ancestors. I was impressed by the efforts made by the US/ Hungarians to keep their traditions alive and to teach their children to have pride in their heritage. However, one comment made by a Hungarian man really struck me!

He said that our heritage is a treasure! I thought that was very well put and it made me realize how far removed many Americans are from their heritage. Not only heritage, but race as well! I believe our race is also a treasure which I see melting away.

Eva Herman a German journalist and talk show host was fired in 2007 for commenting on the good family values during the Nazi era. But, because of the extreme sensitivity that Germans and especially German Jews have regarding this subject a positive can't even be mentioned without condemnation! If read objectively and in context one will see that Eva was not praising the Nazis, but family values during this period. Many will argue that the motivation during this time was the building up of the supposed master race and producing needed cannon fodder for future conquests?

There is truth to both of these points in regards to the Nazis, but I believe that the German people did have strong cultural and family values regardless! Unfortunately the trend now days among many Germans is to distance themselves in every way from this period. Even from the good things! The Nazi's did create the Autobahn and the Volkswagen (people's car). It was Hitler's attempt to provide everyone with inexpensive transportation. The ancestor of our space program stems from German scientists.

A majority of the Nobel prizes have gone to Germans and I am just scratching the surface. There are a great many good things about the German, English and Scandinavian peoples! They are extremely neat, clean, punctual, organized and intelligent. They love order (for the most part) and loathe chaos clutter and disorder! Even the Americans during WW2 admired how well the German people cleaned up after bombing raids, where other countries left their homes and streets a mess.

Many cultures live in total filth, disorder, chaos and anarchy! This is undeniable! Somalia is a prime example! Somalia and many other African Nations are countries in name only and do not have a secure system of government. Gangs and warlords basically run these countries! Tormenting, raping, robbing and dismembering the innocent citizens of these nations! The argument here would be that this is an economic problem.

However, if you moved some other cultures to this region I have no doubt that they would utilize and organize what resources are available and put together an organized form of government. They would adjust their population to the amount of resources available, whereas the current population continues with unbridled procreation. Leaving behind starving un-educated children to fend for their self's. An interesting experiment would be to move the entire population of Switzerland to Somalia and the entire population of Somalia to Switzerland and see what happens given the same resources?

Mogadishu, Somalia

Lucerne, Switzerland

I have no doubts that the Swiss would clean that mess up! With-in a few years most of the buildings would be renovated or re-built and engineered. There would be clean streets, newly formed gardens, parks and a healthy agricultural community. There would be a clean water supply, clean cafes and restaurants, public sewers, good functioning schools and prosperous business and industry. There would be museums, libraries and civic centers, health care, hospitals, police and a public transportation system. Regardless of the lack of resources the Swiss would find a way to efficiently utilize the available resources and form a well-oiled country without, crime, violence or filth. The geographical location would not be nearly as desirable as Switzerland, but I am confident that they would find a way to make this barren land usable and even prosperous.

You might say that the Swiss are more educated and have architects, engineers and good political planners. Well, this may be true, but why have they become more educated, prosperous and organized? Is it just because of their geographical location on the earth and their neighbors? Maybe there is just a difference based on their genetic makeup? I believe that even if you did not send civic engineers, architects, politicians or professors to a land like Somalia, the Swiss are still neat and organized people and would not tolerate the current living conditions.

Germany is roughly the size of Montana, yet they manage over 82 million people with a good quality of life, a high standard of living and they have one of the top 5 largest economies on earth. Pretty impressive for a nation of their size! They are environmentally conscious and maintain forests, parks and rural areas. They balance the economy with prosperous industry and a low unemployment rate. The average time off for workers in Germany is six weeks as opposed to the average two weeks in the U.S. They have cultural centers, museums, arts, sports and a high quality of education. Most of Western and Northern Europe has similar traits. However, the problem with many first world countries is that they freely allow immigrants from third world countries to enter and make themselves at home; which in some cases causes erosion from with-in.

This has become a major problem in many European countries. In modern times we try so hard to be politically correct, that we glance over the potential problems and welcome with open arms! To do otherwise would be racist and politically incorrect! I am by no way implying that third world immigrants should be banned from entering first world countries altogether, but we need to take a hard serious look at the negative consequences that **will** result from this open arms policy. A much harder stance must be taken when we choose to allow immigrants into these countries!

Switzerland's former Justice Minister Christoph Blocher and leader of The Swiss Peoples Party wanted to impose restrictions on the amount of immigrants allowed in the country and to deport immigrants and their families who have committed crimes. He is called an extremist and has been accused of racism. The left wing says his policies promote xenophobia! Christoph says he wants to protect his country from the escalating crime rate caused by foreigners. This is also a problem in Germany and the Scandinavian countries. Many people, especially foreigners see this as a big red flag and something to be very concerned about!

Whenever a crackdown on crime, race or immigration is addressed the race card is quickly pulled and there is almost always immediate opposition! It is usually viewed as something more sinister than it really is or might be? In light of our world history this makes perfect sense! People start to think of the Nazi's and their extreme racial policies or the United States and the past treatment of blacks and American Indians or the internment of the Japanese during World War 2. These are such dark chapters in world history that it has stunted all reasonable thought in regards to balance. Again I go back to my first statement where I addressed the fear of doing anything that might be construed as racist! As a result the floodgates have been opened and you better not offend anybody!

Chapter 2

Extremes

I too am sickened by the extremist racial policies of the past. I think the treatment of the Jews by the Nazi's was almost incomprehensible! What a living nightmare that must have been? When I think of families being ripped apart and sent to ovens, I am horrified! Especially the innocent children who don't understand any of it? When I think of how a Jewish boy must have felt when going to school with Hitler youth kids and being mercilessly teased and harassed because he did not fit the mold it breaks my heart! That is some serious hate!

That kind of extremism is totally unacceptable and should continue to be fought against! The same applies to how mercilessly the blacks and American Indians were treated during white expansion and during and after slavery. The problem though, is that NOW, we are on the other extreme! Give them what they want, don't offend anybody, open our borders to one and all, ignore inappropriate behavior because of race, give people special distinctions, pay reparations to everyone indefinitely, etc., etc.! This is the other extreme and it is also un-acceptable!

We need to be realistic and truthful! We need to remember the past, but we can't change it, and the current population should not be criticized for the doings of our ancestors. We need to call it what it is! A criminal is a criminal and some cultures and races simply DO commit more crimes than others. 1/3 of all black males in the US end up in prison at some point in their lives. That is huge and can't be blamed on poverty and prejudice alone. Martin Luther King Jr. said a man should be judged on his character and not the color of his skin, but when blacks are committing a majority of the violent crimes it makes it hard. Even non-white races think blacks are dangerous based on experience with them. Ask any Asian who owns a convenience store in the inner city.

Other cultures and races live in filth! The Muckleshoot Indians of Western Washington in the United States, although relatively non-violent, are notorious for the clutter and filth they live in! Whether this is cultural, racial, environmental, social, economic, and genetic or whatever, it is what it is! I think that the Christoph Blocher's of the world should take a stand and try to preserve their country! Assuming of course that they are not on the other extreme!

Chapter 3

Deportation

Whenever, someone suggests deportation of illegal immigrants or legal immigrants who have committed crimes against the host country, many become highly offended. They use words, like racist, xenophobia and intolerance. In the US this is hotly debated.

In February of 2008 on the popular TV program the "O' Reilly Factor" Geraldo Rivera and Bill O' Reilly got into a hot debate on the subject. The debate centered on an illegal alien involved in a drunken driving death. O' Reilly's argument was that had the illegal alien not been here the death would not have occurred. Geraldo said that these kinds of things happen regardless and O' Reilly's views toward illegal immigrants fuels the fire of racism in America. These were not the exact words used by Geraldo, but...he is admittedly not only far left, but...a radical. I do understand both points of view and do not consider myself on the left or the right. Many of my opinions would be considered liberal and many very conservative. However, in regards to Geraldo I get the impression that he is OK with illegal's storming the border.

His argument is that at the turn of the century Irish, Germans and Swedes were coming to America in mass migrations, but that was viewed as acceptable back then; Where, now that the Mexicans are coming over in mass migrations, many people see it as un-acceptable. This he sees as racist and intolerant. O' Reilly reminded him that the Europeans were coming over through Ellis Island as **legal** immigrants and at that time American needed people with skills. Geraldo also does not mention that there was hostility even towards newer European immigrants from their more established predecessors.

My view is obviously closer to O' Reilly's than Geraldo's. I feel that back then America was not heavily populated and did need skilled workers as well as laborers to help build America.

I see the present immigration from Mexico as adding huge masses of un-skilled and illegal aliens. There is a big difference to the immigration patterns of the past and present. The past immigration at the turn of the century helped

America. However, the current trend of immigration hurts America, because of the level of saturation from 3rd world nations and the illegal element.

If Mexicans came over legally and brought with them a skill, then they would be viewed much differently. However, many are illegal and suck our economy dry. This is also very unfair to the Mexicans who came over legally and learned the language. Now the legal, former Mexican citizens have to compete for dwindling jobs with the illegal Mexicans. Is this fair?

In Gerald's book His-panic he brags about how hardy the Mexicans are and how we should want them on our side. I agree that most are very hard workers and motivated. However, you need to look at where they are economically. They are harder and more motivated workers right now, because they come from an impoverished country. Once they become assimilated through a generation or two, and are enjoying the fruits of The United States they become just like a lot of other Americans; they get more comfortable, softer, fatter and lazier.

In fact you see it all the time now, well-assimilated fat Mexicans. Everyone works harder and has more motivation when they are under pressure. Not just because they are Mexican. When the Irish immigrants came over during the potato famine they were hard working and motivated too, because they were starving! Anything was better than where they came from and they were forced to survive!

In regards to African Americans, I can guarantee that if they stopped with the gangster rap image that they have created for themselves by their controversial rap lyrics and crime, glorifying guns and violence and became hard working respectful citizens, who wore proper fitting clothes and spoke proper English, they would be treated with much, much more respect! Its the attitude and not the race that create prejudice! They seem to feel that the only way they can get respect is through fear and by intimidation. But just because you are feared doesn't give you respect!

If illegal aliens did not sneak across the border from Mexico, people would have more respect for them. Breaking laws is the act of a criminal, not someone who wants change and real respect. I certainly don't want to generalize different races, because a majority of African Americans and Mexicans are good people and it is a shame that a few ruin it for the rest and give their race and culture a bad name! I work with several Mexicans and there is not one that I don't like or respect.

I saw a program about Hospitals along the border and how many were going bankrupt because of all of the illegal immigrants crossing the border and needing health care. These hospitals can't refuse to give many kinds of treatment regardless. So, in effect these hospitals are going out of business. One illegal immigrant was interviewed and I was shocked at how she viewed the situation. When asked her feelings of how she and others like her were bankrupting hospitals along the border by not being able to pay for treatment and not being a citizen she said;

"Americans are rich and educated; they can afford to take care of us. We are not rich and educated and cannot afford it" Basically saying that what she is doing is OK, because we are better off. Yes, we are better off and yes; I have sympathy for many of the hard working Mexicans who just want a better life. However, The US cannot maintain an endless supply of legal or illegal immigrants into this country who take and don't give anything back. I resent that this continues to be called a race issue. This is an issue of US survival.

We might be wealthier and more educated with better schools and health care, but we are not invincible! We cannot maintain an endless supply of immigrants from 3rd world nations! America is divided in their views. Many are humanitarians and want to help everyone. I respect this unselfish attitude, but on the same hand we can no more successfully help everyone in need any more than the little old lady who keeps collecting stray cats and dogs. Eventually there will be so many that they will destroy the house, the yard and deplete the little old ladies income to where she cannot afford the food or health care for herself or those animals.

It is my firm belief that the US should only take immigrants who help America. It does not matter from which country they come from as long as they are a benefit to the country and are not a hindrance. I don't think the US should have to take any immigrants if they are not needed even if they have skills to bring. If they are a benefit and needed then they can come. This is not the 19th century where immigration was needed. With a population of over 300 million, we have enough people already!

Illegal immigration is hurting everybody. It hurts legal immigrants because they have to compete with illegal immigrants for jobs, which in effect will limit the pay both get. It hurts Illegal immigrants because they will never be above board and will always be forced to work hard labor for low pay. It hurts everyone else in America too, because the cost associated with paying their medical bills and the tax supported social benefits they use, not to mention the added crime, increased population and pollution.

They don't pay for it, but they strain our police force, freeways, schools and hospitals. Many Mexicans are good people who just want to make a better life for themselves. However, by coming here illegally they are like a cancer infecting and undermining America. If they just put in the extra work to be here legally they could aspire to be more than just common labors working for low pay generation after generation! Many drop out of school by the 9th grade and end up in gangs or working hard all their life for peanuts.

Many of these illegals are overpopulating the planet. They have no control when it comes to childbirth. They don't seem to exercise birth control at all. These next few statements will seem inhuman, but I see this view as being more humane than any other. We do not have an over population of stray cats and dogs running around in most cases because we have them neutered or spayed. If we did not have the responsibility to manage this problem then there would be major health problems.

London use to have a huge problem with stray cats, but now it is managed. Now I am obviously not suggesting sterilization of people, but there is this little thing called birth control and this is not inhuman! People know how to not have so many kids! Some first world countries use birth control and maintain their populations and economies just fine. Sorry folks there cannot be endless growth! We are depleting our resources and destroying the environment because of this way of thinking! Planning a family will save our resources, the natural environment, reduce crime and significantly reduce the risk of wars between nations, which are often a result of competition for resources.

In Geraldo Rivera's book Hispanic, Geraldo goes on and on about how the mass influx of the Latino population is one of the greatest things to happen to America. He brags about how in the 1950's there was only about 4 million Latinos and now there are approximately 45 million. He brags about one illegal student in particular that graduated with a 3.9 GPA in Colorado, but could not get state funded tuition because he was illegal. Geraldo thought that this was the real crime and totally glanced over the fact that this person was an illegal alien. He goes on and on about how the system is holding illegal aliens back and how unjust it is, as if the system is criminal! I fully understand that it was not the students fault he was put into this situation, but rather the fault of his parents who came over illegally in the first place, and I have no doubt that this person would have been an asset to the U.S. However, I have a few questions for Geraldo,

Now, why are these people here illegally again?

Why should it be OK to let undocumented people flood into America?

Why should U.S. citizenship, ID cards, health care and other benefits just be given out to anyone who sneaks in?

And....Why can't these illegal immigrants just follow the legal path to citizenship???

These are questions he really does not address. He knows what they are doing is wrong just as much as everyone else does, but in my opinion he is bias, because he shares some Hispanic ethnicity. Examples of Hispanics who are an asset to American still does not make it right to be illegal? How is this justified? Nor are white Americans who complain of illegal emigration necessarily racist as he claims. There are just as many blacks and other races including Hispanics who complain about illegal immigration.

If Hispanics were following the legal process there probably would not be a debate over the subject. There really can be no argument if someone follows the rules and becomes a legal citizen. The reason there is so much hostility regarding this topic is simply because of the attitudes of the illegal aliens. Many do not even attempt to go the legal route, because it is too hard, so they opt for the path of least resistance. They just want to sneak in and take advantage of the benefits of the U.S. without going to the trouble of learning about the country and learning the language.

His book "Hispanic" addresses the fear many Americans have of the changing face of the United States, A face that he encourages and embraces, as if the flood of illegals will one day liberate the U.S. from the white oppressors and this will become a Hispanic nation! Yes, some of our white ancestors were oppressive, but others also formed this great nation with all of its freedoms and they drafted the constitution that makes this country so great! The Hispanic peoples did not create this nation! They did not draft the constitution or create the free enterprise system. They love this country for what it stands for and the limitless opportunities, and that is why they flock to it! But many like Geraldo ironically seem to hate the very people who created it?

If the Hispanic people are so hardy, hardworking, dedicated, determined and intelligent, then why don't they change their nation and turn it into a fabulous country like the United States of America?

This nation didn't come without a fight! And our forefathers were just the right kind of men and women to make the dream of a United States of America become a reality! Are the current Mexicans the right kind of people to take their nation to a better tomorrow or are they the kind of people who will just abandon it for a country already established in a free democracy? The people of Mexico need to unite and fight against their corrupt government. They need to take the ideas they like from the U.S. and implement them into their own country! If they choose this route the world will be a better place and the Mexicans a prouder race of people!

Geraldo is unfortunately probably correct; this great land that immigrants from all over the globe flock to will most likely, eventually become predominantly Hispanic. For a time the Hispanic peoples can rejoice in their victory! However, shortly they will notice that the descendants of the people who masterminded this great nation with all of its freedoms and liberties will be gone! They will look around for someone to take the reins when this new land starts to look more and more like the land they fled so many generations ago....but it will be too late!

History gives countless examples of great civilizations like Rome, Egypt and Greece who eventually fell to the pressures from hordes of dissatisfied peasants and barbarians, leaving in their wake the dark ages that followed. From what it looks like the U.S. will not learn from the mistakes of these great empires and will follow the path to destruction like the great nations before it! The masses of Hispanics will invade, procreate, intermix and nibble away at the population until they are all that is left. That is how the Roman Empire met its demise. Now don't get me wrong, all of these empires had evil aspects about them. However, they also had good, and the barbarians who eventually ate away at them until they became extinct were no better when it came to the treatment of the common people and they were no strangers to evil! As much as people complain about the injustices of the U.S., one day they will be longing for the good old days!

Geraldo gives countless examples of how legal and illegal Hispanic immigrants have overrun this town or that city over the years and how the population is spreading unbridled as if it is a good thing? He does not seem to give any thought to other races, but the one he is a part of, so who's the racist? He seems to brag about how the Hispanics have overrun what use to be predominately black neighborhoods, white neighborhoods, and Asian neighborhoods and how in 100 years they will dominate the nation as they already do in many areas, as if no other races matter but the Hispanic races.

He treats other races as if they have unwarranted fears toward the Hispanic peoples and how they are a wonderful benefit to the nation, yet in the same breath he explains how at the current rate they will in fact be the dominate force in America and over run every other race. **That's what our panic is Geraldo!** Maybe some of us value our ethnicity as you do yours and don't want to be dominated by the never-ending influx of Hispanics. Don't get me wrong, I truly enjoy the color and diversity of this nation, but don't want to be dominated either and want my cultural and racial identity to live on! I am sure many others feel the same as I do, but that does not make them a racist because they have an appreciation of who they are and don't want to lose their identity any more than you do! Races and cultures are treasures to be preserved!

No, I don't hate Hispanics, blacks, Jews, Indians, Pacific Islanders, Asian, Russians, Germans, Irish, Scandinavians, Muslims or the French! However, this used to be a nation of diversity. When I say diversity, I am talking about having different cultures, races and religions, not mixing them all together in one unidentifiable soup!

Here is an example of what I am talking about; I have a nephew who has blonde hair and blues eyes and because of the mass influx of Hispanic people into the area in recent years, he is the only white boy in his class. I went to school in this same area and the ratio was much different then. There were children of all races, but things were more balanced. Today the ratio is staggering.

Now tell me, what chance does he have to keep his ethnicity alive in this environment? He almost does not have any choice of mate other than Hispanic. When he has children with his most likely option they will take on the dominant features of the Hispanic race. Black Americans will eventually melt away with-in the dominant Hispanic population too, because they are fewer in number compared to the Hispanics. I am sure Geraldo is delighted by the almost certainty that all other races will melt away into a pool of Hispania.

I don't dislike Hispanic people and would be one of the first to agree that most are hard workers just looking for a better life. The ones that I know and work with are outstanding individuals! However, I also think that there would not be such a dominance of Hispanics if we addressed the illegal immigration problem. The flow of immigrants will definitely slow way down if you take the illegals out of the equation and the emigrants that make it here legally will in most cases be the most honest, intelligent and disciplined of the immigrants adding a better and stronger strand to the American fabric. The flow is only so heavy because the consequences are so small and the payoff is so big.

Here is the mentality of many illegals. Some might deny this, but in their hearts and minds they know it is true! Just sneak over and pop out some Anchor babies on American soil to sure up your place in America. Work under the table jobs and forget about doing things the legal and proper way. Once you have established some roots and you have enrolled your kids into public schools after a few years the heat will blow over and what politically correct government is going to deport an established family, especially one with kids born on American soil and enrolled in American schools? Thanks to the good old 14th amendment if a child is born on U.S. soil they automatically become a U.S. Citizen.

That is what illegals are banking on and it is very logical, but also very wrong. If the government seriously started deporting illegals there would be a massive out cry of protest by the liberals. They would scream about how inhumane and unfair the government is. I admit it does seem very harsh to deport a child born on American soil illegally and enrolled in an American school. Although the child is legal, if the parent is not, then logically they have to go too so they can be with the mother and father.

I admit that this does seem inhumane! But, again, this is just the mentality and strategy that the illegal parents are using to accomplish their goals. It would be very hard to convince me or anyone else that these immigrants are totally unaware that what they are doing is illegal. And because of this fact the penalty should be harsh. That will be the only thing that will stop this activity. The same principle applies to children. If they break the rules and you throw out idle threats, then the rules will continue to be broken because there is no follow through. The first or second time a parent really follows through on a punishment the less likely the child will continue to break the rules. Of course to the child the parent seems so unfair!

Geraldo gives some great examples of what I am talking about. He will mention a young girl who buys a forged document and fake ID. She illegally sneaks across the border and over time marries a legal citizen of the U.S. and has children; All the while never herself attaining legal status. Then one day ICE comes crashing through her door and tries to deport her. What about the children the liberals cry? The church rushes to the scene to offer a safe haven for the poor victim, celebrities condemn the president and his policies and compare him to Hitler and the sob story continues, protests commence and liberal violence breaks out! All the while people forget that this supposedly innocent victim made these choices all on her own. She choose to buy fake ID and falsified documentation, she choose to enter a country illegally and she choose to get married and have kids, lots of kids to secure a place in the promise land! This is premeditated! She knows full well that if she goes through this process, especially with the anchor babies, the government would look like the devil if they tried to remove her. And you know what? She's right!

I understand that it can sometimes take years to become a citizen and that there are a lot of dynamics and red tape involved, but if I wanted to become a citizen of a country I would do whatever it took. If it became unfeasible then I would have to except that!

I might want to become a citizen of Russia, but if they would not let me in what can I do about it? I certainly would not break the law and force myself upon them! And if I did then I would deserve the consequences! And in Russia I am sure they would be severe! I also understand that some countries have civil wars going on and people are being massacred. If that were the case and I could not get in legally, I might try to sneak in for the sake of survival. However, that is not the case in Mexico. Yes, they are poor, but they manage and can improve upon their life there. They are also not in eminent danger like is the case in some places like Uganda, Rwanda or Somalia.

There is escalating violence with drug lords in recent years, but that is only fairly recent and the U.S. should assist with this problem as a means to secure our borders and safeguard our nation.

My fiancée is Hungarian and grew up behind the iron curtain. She has been a U.S. citizen for approximately 27 years, but the odds were long and the journey a hard one. After spending nearly a year in a refugee camp with some very undesirable characters and having to endure some extremely unpleasant circumstances she was finally allowed into the U.S. She said that only a few families out of the thousands of European immigrants in her refugee camp were allowed entry into the United States, and she believes that the only reason she was allowed entry was because her husband was a gypsy. Her marriage did not last long after her arrival and she was left as a single teenage mother, not knowing a word of English and having a young daughter to care for. She was extremely lonely and probably a little frighten too at the prospect of surviving in a strange land. Someone even advised her to take the easy road by putting her daughter up for adoption and finding a rich American to marry.

Appalled at the thought of this, she wrote an ad which she used a English/Hungarian dictionary to translated. It said that she would work for free making coats on a trial basis. Soon she was getting a paycheck, but still barley managing to support herself and her young daughter. Her father wanted her to come home, but she was a hard working and determined young woman! She learned 5 new English words a day, started taking progressively harder and harder English courses until she mastered the language, earned U.S. citizenship, went on to college and earned a master's degree.

This is a true success story and the type of immigrant who ads a stronger fiber to the fabric of America. This is an example of an immigrant who made it here as a long shot and took full advantage of the opportunity. Yet, we have surpluses of 3rd world immigrants who have been here illegally for decades and whom still barley speak any English and many politicians want to give these people amnesty. Why do some want to give amnesty to a surplus of lower quality immigrants whom came here illegally and make it extremely difficult for those immigrants who do everything right? I have a few theories, like the absurdity of political correctness, liberal propaganda and more votes for the Democratic Party!

In my opinion many politicians are undermining this great nation for personal gain and they are using political correctness and negative racist propaganda to push their agenda and to get their way.

Chapter 4

Extremes vs. Balance

The Nazi's and the current terrorists, who kill the innocent, are and were the extremists! This is pretty clear-cut! However, the people that want to preserve their country, culture and I dare to say it, even race should not be lumped into this category! This is where balance should come in! Things should not be too hard, but certainly not too soft either!

A country like Switzerland is known for its neutrality, beauty, cleanliness and organization. It is known for its race of people that look Swiss and act Swiss! It is known for its quaint and clean little villages and its traditions! It is a beautiful place to see and experience! It is an international country too! People from all over the world are welcome here to visit, study, do business and experience Switzerland! However, when policies are too soft and allow everyone from anywhere to stay permanently, then this is no longer the Switzerland that we know and love!

Look at what has happened in France. There are mobs of blacks and Arab immigrants running wild vandalizing the French suburbs because they feel France is not integrating them well enough. They feel they are not being offered as many opportunities as other French citizens. For one, why do they feel they are entitled to come to a foreign land and expect anything? Why don't they go back to their own homeland? Because it is crap, that's why! So they go to someone else's country and expect to be provided the same jobs, social benefits and opportunities as the native people. If they succeed they will turn the host countries into crap too! If they don't like the way things are then go protest in their own country and make the changes there! Don't come to someone else's country and feel you should have any entitlement! The Mexicans will eventually start rioting in the streets of the U.S. The more you give them the more they expect until there is total anarchy!

When polices are too soft, then criminals flourish and other cultures and races take up residence permanently. This takes away from what is Swiss, French, Scandinavian, German, etc.! If this stance was taken then instead of seeing a Switzerland of Alpine climbers in leder hosen yodeling in the Alps and a blonde blue eyed Heidi wandering the Alpine meadows picking flowers, you might wander through the country and see Mosques, Americanized gangster rappers cru zing the streets in their pimped out rides playing loud rap music, drive by shootings, Buddhist temples or taco Delmar. I am not trying to imply that all of these things are bad, but some are and others have their place and belong to different cultures and regions of the world!

I love to go to a Hawaii, see a Hawaiian luau and see Hawaiian girls dancing in hula skirts! That's what I expect to see when I go to Hawaii. When I go to Switzerland I want to see a Swiss culture or if I visit Africa I want to see that culture, Mexico, Russia, etc., etc.! You will get a little bit of all cultures in most parts of the world and that is OK! But, again I stress balance! This is what is important! This is why it is important to implement some boundaries! Why it is called racist and extremist to try to preserve your country, race and culture in Switzerland? I don't know? Well…. Actually, I do! It is because this is a white culture and white cultures are now days condemned for the slave trade, the Nazi's, the inhuman treatment of the American Indians and the past transgressions of some of our white ancestors.

This is all getting ridiculous and we need to let go of this and start preserving and appreciating the good things that every race and culture has to offer! We also need to condemn the bad! Plus, third world countries want our lifestyle and prosperity, so they are forcing themselves upon us and we are letting them.

What we are heading for is inundating first world countries with third world immigrants. Third world countries don't have to worry about first world countries inundating their nations, because not many people want to go there!

Now this statement is really going to sound racist, but it is undeniably TRUE: Races and cultures are different, that is why some races and cultures are successful and some are not! The mentality and values of some are completely different than others. If you mix these races and cultures together on a large enough scale, then there will be total chaos! What is happening in France is a prime example! The more a country acquiesces and gives these immigrants what they want, the more they will ask for and the worse it will get! Immigrants are OK, to an extent! But, when you start to get mobs of them rioting in the streets and destroying the culture and race of the host countries, then they become a parasite and a cancer that eats up a country from within! I compare some of these immigrants with spoiled children. You give them nice things because you love them and want to help them and make them happy! Then they spit in your face, tell you they hate you and say it is not good enough! Demanding that you give them even more and better as they simultaneously abuse the parent! Weak parents give into the spoiled child and give them what they want. This never helps! They just become more and more undisciplined and rude! Making the parents job a living hell! Now, a good parent would set boundaries and rules. A good parent would also enforce these rules! An extremist parent would grab them by their hair, beat the shit out of them and throw them the fuck out!!!

Hitler was the extreme parent! We are the weak parents and we need to become the strong parents who set boundaries and rules and enforce them! If they are not followed then the child is punished accordingly. Children need to be shown love and encouragement, but sometimes they need tough love when their behavior gets out of hand. Children will respect you for being firm, but also for being fair!

It is also easier to be a good parent and enforce the rules if you don't have 12 kids too! 1-4 are manageable, but the bigger the numbers the greater the chaos in some cases! This applies to immigration as well and the type and amount we allow into our countries! However, there are some very good families with many children! People that really value family and who see having a lot of kids as a blessing like the Mormons. I am personally not a Mormon and question some of their practices, especially after seeing the movie "September Dawn" but as far as family unity goes, many are experts and have large organized loving families where everyone helps! I am not talking about these types. I am referring to the millions of people who have child after child and can't and don't want to care for them properly!

Why do third world peoples want to immigrate into first world countries anyway? Well, the answer is pretty obvious! Good jobs, organization, industrialization, great opportunities, quality of life, standard of living, quality of education, great medical and social programs, etc. However, first world-industrialized countries can in no way maintain every impoverished third world immigrant who wants to take up residence without reducing their culture, race and current quality of life. This is very obvious, but because of our politically correct societies and compassion for others less fortunate than ourselves, we have a strong desire to fix the world's problems by inviting them to take up residence or not protecting ourselves from them taking up residence!

One of the biggest disgraces is the lackluster attempt on the part of the U.S. to secure our borders! We are the lone Super Power and have held off Japan, the Nazi's and mighty Russia, but we can't hold off a basically un-armed invasion of the third world.

An atomic strike will probably not be our downfall, but a slower invasion from the third world! Illegal immigrants are being provided with identification cards in some states and receiving social benefits. Mexican mothers in the U.S. Legal and illegal average **3.5** children and an estimated 200,000 to 400,000 are crossing our borders every year. The hope and belief with many Americans is that we can bring those people up to our quality, when in fact we will **reduce** our overall quality in every area.

It won't be long before we are a minority and our say will be muted. We will have been conquered and will be without a voice substantial enough to make a change! When we do raise a voice it will be slammed down as racist! Many Mexicans actually feel there should be an open border policy. Can you imagine how bad things would be if that were the case? Mexicans themselves would not like the overall result of us doing that. The reason is that the land of opportunity would dry up and the US would begin to resemble the country they fled. Mexico is not impoverished so much because of the land, but because of how the land is managed, a ridiculously high birth rate and a poor government.

Los Angeles County is an example of what the United States might look like in the not so distant future? According to the US census Bureau and www.davickservices.com, an on demand mobile abstracting and public records Research Company, the population there is over 71% minority as of August 15th, 2007. In fact the total minority population in LA County alone according to the above sources exceeds the total population in 38 of our 50 states! These statistics are staggering! I checked and rechecked this information to make sure it was accurate, because to me it is almost unbelievable!

To me these statistics are very scary and extremely depressing! Not because I don't like minorities, I like everybody, but because I feel like my race and culture is being swallowed alive! I personally would not mind being a minority in my own country if I had the satisfaction of knowing that others like me valued and were committed to preserving their ethnicity! Not because I think my race is necessarily better than any other race, but, **because it is my race!**

From my viewpoint and from what I can see all around me is that even many whites do not value or appreciate their race! They have no problems marrying a minority and forfeiting their blood forever. Blood or heritage seems to have no value to many whites. In fact I think many people don't think that being white is too cool anymore. This is obvious by how the white kids (wangsters) are dressing like and emulating their heroes in the hood. If you put some of those spoiled middle class kids in the hood for a day, I guarantee they would change their tune real quick, if they survived? It is depressing to me that some of the worst people are the ones that our youth idolize the most? There was a day when people valued someone who was polite and courteous, someone loving and faithful, and someone clean and clean cut, respectful, intelligent and disciplined. To idolize people that would burn down your house with you and your family in it and then laugh about it is sickening. To idolize people that have no trace of decency or morality is confusing to me? When they are not rapping and robbing people, they are guilty of smaller offenses like throwing crap out the window and painting graffiti all over the place and their language and actions has reached unprecedented forms of vulgarity and cruelty.

Exaggerated or not, here might be a typical day in the life of a gangster in the hood: Wake up at 3:00pm, crack open a 40 oz. Bottle of Old E for breakfast, greet your neighbor by saying "what the fuck you looking at you mother fucking bitch ass ho", school? Fuck that shit! Unless you're going to sell some drugs, kill somebody or pick up a ho? Do a few crunches, shove your 9mm in your baggy ass pants with a red or blue belt to keep them falling too far below your crotch, go sell some crack to the kids at the park, rape your neighbors wife and rob her too, throw your Old E out the window to break in the local park where the kids play, meet your homies at Mickey D's, push a few patrons out the way, tell the clerk to get you a fuckin Big Mac and some fries (don't pay for it), cuss at a few more people as you knock them the fuck out the way, throw your litter everywhere and pay special attention to smearing the ketchup all over the place, go to the rest room and take a shit on the toilet, not in it, so people can see how foul you are, write or paint some vulgar shit on the walls, beat somebody's ass with the help of many of your compadres to make sure there is a total unfair advantage, go to the next neighborhood and do a drive by and then get totally hammered at a party repeating this behavior until dawn, then sleep again till 3:00 pm. What a world it would be if everyone were like this.

If everyone were like that there would not be a convenience store to rob, a car to drive to the drive by or a school to sell drugs at, etc. The people who do contribute to society are the ones who make the gangster life possible, by providing products to steal and hardworking tax paying citizens to rob.

I know that the above paragraphs are offensive and a horribly exaggerated, comical stereotypical view of gangs in the inner-city overall, but there are people who behave precisely in this way! Maybe not in that exact order, but you know what I mean! The lack of morals, values, common courtesy and human decency among some people are what's offensive!

I was at the Laugh Factory in LA with recently and there was a black female comedian. She had slightly lighter skin than your average black, but she was definitely black. She even looked like she had blue eyes? Anyway, she mentioned that she was half Swedish and half black. She also mentioned that after one of her shows a couple of black women came up to her and said "Honey, your no Swede, your black! Once you have a single drop of black blood in you, then you're black!" So, I guess it is true! Once you go black you can't go back, lol!

I mean what can you say about a topic as controversial as this? There will be so few people on my side about this particular subject! I mean so, many people intermix now days. There are attractive men and women of all races, so it's hard to resist! Especially since the dark minority population is so high these days. Some people have trouble finding a mate period, let alone being so picky as to only date with-in their race! And if you're a white person living in LA County with 71% minorities, you're almost shit out of luck!

I myself was personally married to a woman of a Philippine, Indian and white mixture and dated a Puerto Rican girl in college. I never had kids with my Philippine wife, but I remember how people would comment on how attractive our kids would be. I was 6'3", and athletic with blond hair and blue eyes and she was 5'2" and was very unique looking in her own right being a mixture of so many races. I have no doubt that our kids would have been attractive. However, they would resemble her dominant race more than mine, because dark features almost always prevail!

She looked like her father who was half Philippine and half Tlingit Indian, but showed very little resemblance to her white mother who was Irish, Scottish and Welch. Therefore, if you are a pure blooded Swede and you procreate with a black or any other dark race of people; you will have forfeited your race. Now you can say the same for the other person too, but remember, dark genes are dominate, and those traits are not easily over ridden like that of a white person. Look at Barrack Obama for example; he is not considered a white man. Although, his mother is white, people consider him black. Once you go black your white heritage and race are gone forever, but if you're black and intermix your race will still live on!

Chapter 5

Blonde haired Blue-eyed Extinction

Now this chapter is going to sound very racist. However, when read entirely you will see my opinion is not that I dislike any other race, but have concerns about some staggering statistics in regards to race. There are the Heidi Klums of the world who talk proudly of their German heritage and culture, but then procreate with the most opposite race they can find, wittingly or not contributing to the destruction of a race of people. I have noticed this with a lot of Germans. It is much unexpected. However, I sometimes wonder if they are doing it intentionally to distance themselves from their race and the negative racist ideas of the Nazi regime? Maybe it is just a coincidence? This is a hot topic and I am sure Heidi would not appreciate me using her and her ex-husband as an example, but I think special care should be considered when passing on your genes.

Love is what it is and no one should be told whom you can or can't marry. But the responsibility of carrying on a race lies with the individual. With most races this is not an issue since they have the numbers to absorb, but the fair skinned people of the world do not have the numbers or dominate genes to do this given the rapid immigration rates. This is a touchy topic and many people will be offended by it. However, if people don't start caring, then over time races and cultures will begin to disappear! We are trying very hard to save rare animals like the Giant Panda, but fail to see that certain strains within our own human race are already becoming extinct. That may seem ridiculous to many, but if you look at the trends and do the math you will quickly see that things are heading for a major change unless the individual makes some different choices.

In the October 22, 2006 edition of the San Diego Union-Tribune I saw an article by Douglas Belkin titled **"Not many Americans born with blue eyes"** In the article it talked about the 300 millionth American(s) born. It listed four babies born within seconds of each other as contenders for the symbolic title of the 300th million American. Two of the children were African American and the other two were originally from Puerto Rico and Jamaica." The births highlight a trend among Americans: Neither of the babies is likely to have blue eyes." The article goes on to say that: "once the Hallmark of the boy and girl next door, blue eyes have become increasingly rare among American children. Immigration patterns, intermarriage and genetics all play a part in their steady decline. While the drop off has been a century in the making, the plunge in the past few decades have taken place at a remarkable rate."

"About half of Americans born at the turn of the century had blue eyes, according to a 2002 Loyola University study in Chicago. By midcentury the number had dropped to a third. Today only about 1 out of every 6 Americans has blue eyes, said Mark Grant the epidemiologist who conducted the study."

"Grant was moved to research the subject when he noticed that blue eyes were much more prevalent among his elderly patients in the nursing home where he worked than in the general population. At first he thought blue eyes might be connected to life expectancy, so he began comparing data from early 20th century health surveys. Turns out it has more to do with marriage.

"A century ago, 80 percent of people married within their ethnic group, Grant said. Blue eyes-a genetically recessive trait-were passed down, especially among people of English, Irish and Northern European ancestry."

"By mid-century a person's level of education-not ethnicity-became the primary factor in selecting a spouse. As intermarriage between ethnic groups became the norm, blue eyes began to disappear."

"The influx of nonwhites into the United states, especially from Latin America and Asia hastened the disappearance. Between 1900 and 1950, only about 1 in 10 Americans was nonwhite. Today that ratio is 1 in 3."

"Preferences for fair skin and blue eyes stretch back in Europe to at least the middle ages, according to Hema Sundaram, author of "Face Value," a book about the history of beauty. For women in particular, fair skin and light eyes have long been seen as indicators of fertility and beauty."

These traits are disappearing without a doubt and it is my belief that the majority of people do not care. The majority does not have these traits, so why should they? The most frightening aspect of all of this is that the few people who do possess these traits don't even seem to care. I believe that this trend started in large after the Axis defeat in World War 2. So, unpopular was the Nazi's ideology of racial purity after World War 2 that wittingly or unwittingly the stage was set for the extinction of the Nordic race.

Chapter 6

Lebensborn

During the Nazi reign there was a program called Lebensborn. This was a Nazi program to breed the supposed master race. SS leader Heinrich Himmler founded it in 1935. This was a place where children were bred to be the elite of Hitler's 1,000-year Reich. Himmler encouraged women of pure blood to bear blonde, blue or green eyed children with racially pure German soldiers, married or not. Not only German women, but also tall, blonde, blue-eyed women throughout Nazi occupied Western and Northern Europe. One of the highest concentrations of the Lebensborn clinics was in Norway. The Nazi's encouraged German soldiers to have children with women of "Viking" blood.

Lebensborn was originally designed to halt the high rate of abortions in Germany, which rose as high as 800,000 a year in the inter-war years because of a chronic shortage of men to marry after World War 1. It enabled pregnant unmarried women to have their children in a safe environment with all of the necessary social services and medical care to provide for mother and children, plus enabling them to avoid the social stigma by having their children away from home. However, after the war these innocent children were the victims of the cruelest abuse. Many were raped, beaten and mercilessly harassed! They were called SS bastards at age 3 and paraded down the streets to be beaten or to have rotten fruits and vegetables thrown at them; they were hit with sticks and spat upon by the local citizens. They lived a life of shame, humiliation and loneliness for crimes they never committed and were not old enough to even understand!

In addition to the physical and mental abuse they suffered, they were also extremely lonely, insecure and lived a life without the warmth and love of family ties. Many of these children did not know who their mother or father was, because the Nazi's kept their identities secret. They were in many cases totally deprived of love and care. They lived for decades in hushed shame and uncertainty silently wondering if their fathers were war criminals. They paid a terrible price for crimes they did not commit. In my opinion the perpetrators who inflicted this pain upon them were no better than the Nazi's!

It took 60 years before many of the Lebensborn children started to speak out. Many more to this day have no idea that they are Lebensborn children. The Norwegian government who participated in the program finally issued a formal apology, but only now after a lifetime of shame and abuse.

It goes without saying that the Nazi's were extremely evil and inflicted unspeakable horrors upon Europe, but for people to take out their frustrations on innocent children who had nothing to do with any of it makes no sense at all! To this day I believe that consciously or un-consciously these events in world history have had a negative impact on people who had no part in anything Nazi. However, because of ideas associated with the Nazi's it has in effect, I believe, had much to do with the decline of blonde hair and blue eyes and the white race in general.

I believe there is an underlying prejudice still there towards anyone who resembles what Hitler admired in a person including present day post war Germans or people with blonde hair and blue or green eyes. It is certainly much worse for men than women, since tall, blonde, blue-eyed women are always highly desirable regardless, whereas men are considered the war mongers of the world. Unfortunately, because of this underlying stigma Nordic men and women are procreating with each other less and less resulting in the extinction of these traits. Of course this all seems very unscientific, but I am sure many feel as I do, that these unspoken prejudices exist beneath the surface.

Chapter 7

Iceland

There is one country that I really admire and that is Iceland. Icelanders can easily trace their ancestry back to the 10th century. One reason is that they were very isolated for many centuries, but also because they have enormous pride in who they are and where they came from. Even today and they are very unlikely to marry or procreate outside their own race or even their country. In this day and age it is extremely rare to find a group of people as homogeneous as the Icelanders. Some say they are xenophobic because they won't marry outside their race, but I think it is very noble. As the overwhelming majority of the world's dark skinned population continues to overrun Europe and America, and white populations are willingly forfeiting their blood to dark races, it is comforting to know that somewhere in the world there is a small pocket of fair skinned people who actually care about their ethnicity and go to great lengths to preserve it.

The total population is approximately 316,000 and almost all of the men can be traced back to Nordic ancestry during the Viking age through scientific studies such as blood type and genetic analysis and almost all of the women can be traced back to Ireland and are of Celtic origin. It is thought that the Viking marauders stopped by Ireland and picked up some Celtic slave girls for the new settlement? The population is so homogeneous that the Icelandic people are valuable tools for conducting research on genetic diseases.

One study shows that nearly 90% of Iceland's population has blue or green eyes. They also have one of the highest percentages of blonds. Just like a rare gem the Icelandic people are truly like a rare diamond in a sea of coal. If they don't give into the pressure of those who call them xenophobic and continue to preserve their race, and if the European and Americans keep giving away their blood, they will become the last vestige of Nordic blood and a rare sight to behold!

I can see how some people would be easily offended by my praise of Icelanders and I guess it does sound like I am saying these people are diamonds and everyone else is coal. But, really what I am trying to convey, is that they are rare, and there is always a beauty in rare things and this rarity should be protected and preserved, so it does not disappear from the Earth. If diamonds covered the earth like sand then they would not be so special!

Is having the desire to preserve your ethnicity being racist? Some people would say yes, and if that is the case then I think we need to redefine racism. As I have said before there are many races that are white and non-white who firmly believe in the preservation of their race and culture. If you've ever seen the movie "My Big Fat Greek Wedding" you know what I am talking about!

Chapter 8

100 Years of Destruction

Look at what has happened to our world in the last 100 years because of technology! The Write brothers made their first flight just a little over 110 years ago at the time of this writing. Now the skies are full of commercial, personal and military aircraft. 100 or so years ago cars were a rare site and had little or no impact on human life or the environment. Now the streets are choked and the environment is in grave danger as a result! Of course these inventions are a major breakthrough and have changed lives for the better. However, as we are now seeing, these inventions could also change things for the worse!

I am certainly not saying we should go back to the turn of the century life, but am stressing how fast things are changing and the damage that is being done as a result. The change in technology is also changing our racial makeup! The world is becoming a smaller place and as a result people from all races are traveling and mixing which will eventually overtake the more vulnerable fair skinned race of people. Now let me stress that technology and mixed races are not necessarily bad, but without some balance certain ethnicities and the environment could be destroyed.

We are seeing the effects of global warming, the carnage people have brought to the Earth and how people are now addressing ways to reduce pollution and the human impact, and I think it is becoming pretty clear that if changes are not made we can say goodbye to the world as we know it!

As far as preserving particular strains and cultures of the human race are concerned, I think this may be of little concern to many people! This might follow along the lines of urgency of saving the Giant Panda or less? But, I still think the Panda is worth saving as well as our own ethnicities! There won't be much impact on the human race if the Giant Panda goes extinct. However, I still think they are a beautiful and rare breed and should not be allowed to go extinct! I feel the same why about vulnerable human cultures and races.

The life left for red hair is estimated to be only about a hundred years before extinction! For thousands of years these strands flourished, but today the rate of decline is staggering. At the beginning of this century we have gone from about 51 percent of the population having blues or green eyes in the U. S. to now only 1 in 6.

But this is America and Europe for the most part. Some countries, cultures and races never intermix and they don't complain. There is not a need to. At this point the selection of mates within our own race is still available, if you look a little harder and consider passing on your genes on for the future. If you fall in love with someone of another race and you really want to be with that person then there should be no denying you the right. However, in most cases it just happens without too much thought.

I in NO way think that I can change the world's attitudes and actions merely by writing this book. However, I feel strongly enough about it to at least say something, in the hope that some people who possibly were not aware of these staggering statistics might consider what is happening to their ethnicity and make different choices.

This book is not about racism (although that will be hotly debated!) This book is about balance. The world will never be perfect, but in order to preserve our planet and the human race, we will have to balance and manage our population and natural resources. Every decision that will ever be made will step on somebody's toes! If you want to preserve the environment by implementing good forestry practices, you will offend the forestry industry, because the bottom line is profit.

These companies do take measures at preservation, but in reality it is just enough for appeasement! They do just enough to get by and portray an image of care and concern above and beyond just profit. The same is true with the oil companies and every other company involved in pollution making and exploitation for profit. As educated and intelligent as humans are they sure do some pretty stupid things! Power and greed seems to outweigh common sense! We have the intelligence to visit other planets, built hydrogen bombs and have computers that are the size of a pen, yet we cannot or are unwilling to make some easy basic changes to preserve our planet from disaster. The basic changes are, stop polluting the shit out of the earth. We have the technology to build hydrogen cars right now, but because of the greed of the oil companies and their affiliates it is not used. They throw a prototype at us once in a while to give the illusion that they are trying to solve the problem. In my opinion this is just an illusion to milk as much time and money as possible! If they wanted to everyone could be driving gas free cars within a few years.

Here is my biggest pet peeve and the one of the main premises for this whole book; Stop over populating the earth! Instead of spending billions of dollars on figuring out how to provide for the projected population increase, simply stop having so many kids. We have had the birth control technology for decades. However, only the developed countries use it. Germany has reduced its birth rate to 1.39 children per woman, so now the German government is concerned about their birth rates being too low and is now offering incentives for woman to have more children. So, what's the problem then? A saturation of immigration from 3rd world countries and the birth rate in 3rd world countries is the problem! Population reduction will affect the economy adversely for a while, because there will be less people of working age paying into social security and similar programs, but as the older generations naturally die out, we should eventually reach a good and sustainable population.

Chapter 9

The Blame Game

The American Indians were robbed of their life style and land, Africans were kidnapped and taken to a new continent to become slaves and the Jews suffered more than any other race during the wholesale massacre of the holocaust!

Yes, some white people committed a great many sins. But for one, those people are ghosts and the descendants are not responsible for those crimes against humanity. Moreover, I wouldn't blame it on the race.

Romans 3:21 "All men have sinned and shall fall short of the glory of god"

The fact is that humans are innately evil and good! The terrorists and suicide bombers of the mid-east are not white, but carry out horrible acts against innocent civilians, even of their own race and peoples who share their same religion! It is almost certain that some of the thousands who died during 9-11 were Muslims.

African Americans are killing each other every day in drive by shootings and warlords in Africa commit unspeakable horrors to the population there. The Japanese have the rape of Nan king among their many atrocities, the Aztecs have their sacrifices, and the Spanish conquistadors were notorious for their brutality and the Nazi's the most infamous of all!

Race is irrelevant. This evil is a human characteristic and as white people, we should not allow others to make us feel guilty for acts that the ghosts of the past have committed!

My sentiments are with the **preservation** of a vulnerable race of people. Not out of hate of other races or the belief in the superiority of a race of blonde haired, blue or green eyed people or Northern European white people in general as was Hitler's view, but because of the rarity, beauty and uniqueness of this race. Studies show that by the year 2221 blonde hair and blue and green eyed people will be virtually extinct, with the last blonde being born in Finland.

This was at first brought to my attention by a blonde haired blue-eyed woman who was married to a man that was a Pacific Islander. She had three kids with him, none of which resembled her or took on her traits. For some reason she seemed to be delighted by this fact? She mentioned that her husband was attracted to her because of her fair features. Therefore, the people who are to blame for this extinction process are the white people themselves. Although the study she was referring to was proven to be a hoax, since the gene can't disappear. However, if a person with blonde hair and blue eyes procreates with a person with dark features the child will carry on the dominant dark features 3 out of 4 times and the fairer traits will manifest themselves less and less. Look at Barack Obama, his mom is white, but everyone sees Barack Obama as a black man.

Since the end of Second World War and the defeat of Nazi Germany, many Germans, it seems have tried to drown out anything to do with the Nazi's and racism, including deluding their own blood and the Nazi ideology of racial purity. My guess is because this is precisely the opposite of what the Nazi views were? Modern Germans are still condemned to this day for these views as are white Americans because of slavery. What better way to distance yourself from these past negative ideologies, regimes and eras than to dilute your blood and become an international conglomeration of mixed races? And that is precisely what Germany the U.S. and Europe are becoming. Who can call you a racist or associate you with the Nazi's or slavery if you are married to and have children with non-white races?

For someone who had racial purity at the top of his priorities, Hitler's existence probably did the most to damage and kill out the race he supposedly loved. White cultures in Europe and the U.S. are slowing acquiescing to the pressures of those races that were oppressed by whites in the past. We are intermixing so rapidly that seeing a natural blonde haired blue-eyed person is becoming increasingly rare. (The key word is natural) Redheads who are only 2% of the population are even more unusual! The U.S. population is still predominately white. However, the race is becoming more and more diluted and the white population is decreasing, while the Mexican population is increasing rapidly.

I am again in no way saying that any other race or mixture of races is a bad thing, but am trying to bring attention to this topic, so people will stop and think! We have a choice of whom we date, marry and have children with. In this day and age I don't think it is possible not to ruffle some feathers by bringing up this topic, but it's still our choice!

I am not a racist! In fact my personal feeling is that all of the different cultures and races bring spice to humanity! If you have ever been on the Disneyland ride "It's a Small World" The characters are depicted as of uniquely diverse races and cultures. The Mexican scene is very colorful and vibrant, the Asian cultures and races with the beautiful Geisha girls adorn in their elaborate costumes, the Polynesian race and culture with hula dancing girls in grass skirts, the pure race of deeply black African tribesman, the fair skinned blond haired blue eye children of the Scandinavian countries and the red headed Irish and other Europeans. All of these races and cultures are very beautiful and unique! **I think the world would be a very dull place without all of this diversity!**

Many races have nothing to worry about! Asians consist of over 60% of the world's population and a majority of this population is concentrated in Asian countries, so there is virtually no chance of losing pureblooded Asians. On the other end of the spectrum pureblooded Hawaiians are nearly extinct and if it were not for a small island of them sticking together and not procreating outside their race they would become extinct within a few generations. American Indians only comprise of 7% of the U.S. Population and some of the best strains were killed off during the plains wars, the trail of tears where the Native Americans had to endure a horrific forced march to reservations barely suitable for existence and the small pox virus introduced by the Europeans.

Humanity has predominately dark hair, dark skin and dark eyes. There are varying shades, but predominately dark. The nearly 4 billion Asians have black hair, dark skin and dark eyes as do the Africans, most of South America and Mexico (with minor exceptions) India, which is over 1 billion in population, the mid-east and the all of the island peoples; the main areas that are left such as Europe, North America, New Zealand, Australia, etc. Are highly educated, industrialized 1st world countries that do business throughout the world? 500 years ago Europe was fairly isolated and had little contact with other races, but from 1492 onward the Europeans expanded or journeyed into the Americas, the South Pacific, Africa and Asia. The result of this was contact and inters mixing with other races.

This was not the choice of the subjugated races, but nevertheless it happened and is increasing as transportation and communication became more advanced. As a result immigration increased exponentially. Citizens from the poorer third world countries now want to come to Europe and America to live a better life or were brought here un-willingly as slaves many years ago.

Currently in the U.S. illegal aliens are storming across the border from Mexico and now outnumber African Americans. Spanish is practically becoming a second language there has been such an increase. With our Asian, Indian, Mexican and middle eastern immigrants, (to mention a few) plus the population of African Americans, white Americans are inter mixing more and more regularly.

Desegregation in the 1960's although politically correct has also helped increase this trend immensely! Not to mention the sensitiveness of the racial issues that was brought about by Nazism and the slave trade. The industrialized European countries have also experienced mass emigration. There are now more Mosques in Germany than Christian churches. The result is that the dominant dark genes are easily over riding the fair skinned peoples of Europe and America. Many will argue and resent such a fuss about this! After all what's the matter with mixing cultures and races to a point where they are no longer recognizable as different cultures and races? Maybe that is what the world needs? Maybe nice shades of brown where everyone looks similar and where everyone has dark hair, eyes and skin. That way how can there be racism?

This argument sounds logical. However, I honestly don't think it will make a difference? In the Middle East peoples of the same appearance and making are constantly killing each other. The same holds true for Africa. Asia, Europe and most other countries have had their civil wars with peoples of the same making. You don't need race to have prejudice!

Racial and cultural preservation is not just a white issue. In fact most whites are indifferent or unwitting participants to their own extinction. They don't know or they don't care. Maybe they just think it is inevitable, but won't happen in their lifetime, so why fight it? Or they want to distance themselves from their race because of political correctness? In fact most other races are tighter knit and have stronger family, cultural and racial ties than American whites do.

If a white person said they wouldn't marry a person of another race they would undoubtedly be labeled a racist; where it is perfectly acceptable to have this feeling in other races. In fact it is viewed as a noble characteristic and they are admired for their strong family and cultural values!

I think that the white race should have the same pride in whom they are and where they come from! If you have any distinct culture or background left, it should be valued and preserved! People should choose their mates wisely to preserve their ancestry. Most people are curious as to where they came from? If you are white, you can be pretty sure your origins began in Europe. Why not try to preserve that legacy for future generations. Why snuff it out for all time?

I may address my attention a lot to the white race, but that is because I see it as the most vulnerable and disappearing before my very eyes. I am proud of my ancestry. I don't approve of the past transgressions of some members of my race, but I admire the virtues. You can find pluses and minuses in just about all races and cultures, but I choose to focus on the good! If you are German you should focus on the neatness, punctuality, bloodlines, inventiveness, work ethic, culture, intellect and race! Not Hitler and WW2. People who have not traveled extensively may have a picture in their mind as what people look like in different parts of the world. When you think of Swedes, Germans or the Swiss you have a picture in your mind. You might think of the blonde haired blue eyed Swiss miss coco girl and yodeling for Switzerland. However, you might be very surprised when you get there as to what you will find? African Americans are becoming diluted too, although they still have a strong base of pure blood in Africa. Whereas Europe and the U.S. are inundated at the source with other cultures because of their prosperity, leading to racial intermixing.

Not a bad thing in itself if your particular race has the volume to absorb some of that? The Asian population certainly has the volume to absorb as much intermixing, as they want without the risk of losing pure blood. The white race does not, and dark races outnumber whites 6 to 1 and predominately white countries are the most desirable places to emigrate to because of their prosperity, education system, social programs, etc.

So many Americans want to save the world by adopting children from third world countries, but there are far too many…. and what needs to be done is to teach these people how to manage themselves. **"Give a man a fish and feed him for a day… Or teach a man to fish and you feed him for a lifetime"** (Chinese proverb; Lao Tzu) One of the major problems in third world countries is that they have more children than they have the resources to provide for, leading to pain, disease and starvation.

Planning of the births of children and birth control need to be stressed. Our world is only so big and it is extremely unlikely that we are going to find another livable planet to exploit and over populate. Man is spending billions and using some of the world's greatest minds to explore this avenue, when we could just implement management strategies. Management is the key to survival for the human race and our planet. This is another very controversial subject, which will outrage many! However, this is reality! The population is growing at an unsustainable rate. Estimates are that we will reach over 9 billion in population by 2050. Our current population is already drastically effecting the environment. And one day if we don't begin to manage resources and the population we might be faced with a horrible choice, and be following the practices of Adolf Hitler that now days we are sickened by like, **eugenics**, or mass sterilization and worst, forced extermination of those deemed un-worthy of life! Does this sound familiar?

The most humane thing to do is to teach third world countries how to manage their populations in a humane way like birth control or a vasectomy after you have had two children. Teach them how to cultivate their own land and feed themselves. Angelina and Madonna will never be able to adopt all the kids in need. I have heard people say that if they can just help one life that will be enough. However, through management we can help the whole world and everyone in it!

If we open the floodgates to third world countries the whole world will become a third world country! We will be drug down by the sheer weight of numbers! I am amazed at how the U.S. The lone super power cannot control its own borders from third world countries? There are hundreds if not thousands of illegal immigrants walking into the U.S. every day. Cheap labor is highly desired by American companies large and small and I agree that most Mexicans are hardworking people with strong family values whom just want a better life for their families. However, there are criminals among them too and illegal is illegal and in mass numbers the benefits of cheap labor will be over shadowed by the negatives of an over population of laborers and with that will inevitably come more and more crime and unrest!

Chapter 10

Population Control

At one time the birth rate in Mexico City was an average of 7 children per mother, SEVEN! They just kept having more and more kids until the population of Mexico City became flooded, putting a tremendous strain on resources. Recently that trend has slowed way down. Not because of government enforcement, but because the people just started looking around and said "whoa! This is getting out of control! We can't feed all of these kids!

Proving that it is not too difficult to control the population if the education and desire is there! The Mexican government cannot or will not manage its people. Poverty and an excessive birth rate, little or no education and lack of resources is a major problem in third world countries. The solutions are so obvious it is ridiculous; Population, control, education, management, security, de-forestation, the greenhouse effect, pollution and crime. These are the main problems we deal with as a result of striving for endless prosperity!

With **population control** I mean controlling the birth rate to keep a manageable balance. This will be a point of outrage among religious communities, humanitarians and personal beliefs systems, and no argument in the world will convince some societies. However, just because a woman is capable of having 16 or more children, does that mean she should? Is this what god requires of them? Certainly not! I know many Christians that have a household of four and practice birth control. These parents are very religious, but are also logical; meaning that they know that with their available household income they will be able to provide a good life for themselves and for their two children. This means good food, extracurricular activities, such as sports, music lessons, scouts, good education and being able to devote more time to each child. They know they will be able to put money aside for their children's secondary education, go on family vacations or camping trips. Overall have a good quality of life! By having one sibling a child is not deprived of a play mate either.

This comes from **education.** I don't think most third world countries have so many kids because of a belief system. Most of it is from a lack of education and birth control resources. I realize that even if education and birth control was provided to third world countries, they may not use it. They are not use to that and it is unnatural, they are set in their ways or don't care. Some are just ignorant. A life of suffering is all they have ever known and the little pleasure they do get from life is probably sexual. After they get their brief satisfaction they become ignorant as to what comes next or don't think about it? 9 months of pregnancy with no medical care and if the child survives the provisions are not available to care for them.

After the child is born and starving the process starts all over again brining yet another child into the world and the pattern repeats leaving a country of starvation, disease and pain! This is not humane! In fact it is extremely inhumane! The only thought is to have that brief satisfaction. Sterilization might have to become mandatory after two children for some or the implementation of a birth control device or shot, because the welfare of the whole civilization may not be a thought to the individual? I know that this too resembles fascism. However, we need to think of civilization and the world as a whole and stop being self-minded! By doing well for the world environment and all mankind each individual benefits as well as future generations! I guarantee that many individuals, politicians and corporations don't give a shit about future generations.

Make as much as you can and get as much as you can while it lasts is all that is on many minds! Unfortunately far too many people think this way. You may ask yourself why I even care. I care, because I feel that it is our responsibility to leave the world better than we found it!

Education is not only needed for planning a family, but general education and education on how to provide food and housing for themselves. Agriculture techniques and equipment will have to be donated by first world countries as well as construction materials and techniques. These countries must be helped. They need to be educated and taught how to be organized. Once this is achieved the flood of the third world population will not need to overrun the borders of first world industrialized countries like the U.S., Canada and Europe.

They will have the tools and skills to provide for themselves. They will adjust their population to a percentage of their countries resources. This will not come easy since first world countries would be stretching their own resources to accomplish this and with these countries breeding out of control it will be one step forward and three steps back.

The education and population balance will take a great deal of time and must be done simultaneously as resources from governments and volunteer organizations allow. Birth control is step # 1, education in regards to birth control go hand in hand. Education in agriculture, construction and organization are step # 2.

Security is another important issue. Most people are willing to work to make their lives better. However, many would rather rape, rob and pillage what the hard working honest people have obtained. These countries need to be protected and the roaming gangs disarmed. Every country has crime, but some more than others. The U.S. has a tremendous amount of crime, where Japan, England, Sweden and other first world countries do not. Why is this? For one the U.S. is choking on its liberties. Americans have an entitlement attitude.

There are 4th and 5th generation welfare recipients who pump out the kids with no thought of the consequences or they just don't care; kids that are provided for by the government but are not educated and have limited opportunities. Crime is a way of life for them. Drive by shootings, rapes, robberies, intimidation and murder is all part of the game in many inner cities. Extreme measures should be taken to control this situation. FDR never intended welfare to be abused like this.

Chapter 11

Welfare

There should be an ultimatum. Some families never get off of welfare. It is just expected! There should be a time limit for being on welfare. Welfare should use more money to provide resources and education and not just a free hand out! Single women pump out the kids irresponsibly, (in many cases) use welfare, the kids become criminals, dropouts, drug attics or all of the above, adding even more problems to society!

It happens over and over again! There are exceptions. But the government is enabling this, which is slowly bringing down the working class law-abiding citizens who pay to support these people. **If you are on welfare then birth control should be a pre-requisite to receiving it!** Education or job training should also be a requirement. I really think it would be smart if when children reached puberty they would be required to have some sort of birth control implement like an IUD, which could be removed when the child has become an adult who is willing and has the means to start a family.

Family planning! Abstinence should also be taught in the education of our youth. Not only for moral reasons, because that will become an endless debate, but for health and safety reasons. Since abstinence among all youths is very un-likely, then mandatory birth control should be considered, and I don't mean the distribution of condoms! You have to actually use them for that to work! Plus, it promotes teen sex and most kids don't have that kind of responsibility. If you hand a child a condom you might as well say it is ok to have sex.

If you can't care for a child because you are too young, still in school or a drop out and have no means to care for the child then you have no business having one and society should not have to pay for it! Education will work for some, but mandatory birth control will work for all! This will reduce the crime rate, over population and financial strain to the taxpayers. This will also benefit the environment by reducing the strain on natural resources, less pollution and last but not least the unsightly litter that comes from undisciplined, uneducated and uncaring people!

To an immature mind that has reached puberty their only thought is for selfish pleasure or they are a victim. Ideally a man and women should be married, in love, committed, educated and have the financial means to support a child or children! Of course as logical as this is it will be deemed politically incorrect. With the way the world currently works people run around irresponsibly having sex and having kids who in many cases are un-wanted and un-loved.; is this humane? As a result they are thrown into a world of broken families, crime, violence, welfare and poverty!

These next paragraphs will sound fascist, but these ideas should be looked at logically. A 13-year-old child has the right to keep information given to a doctor about sex confidential. They also have a choice to take birth control or not. They can also get abortions or have a baby without a parent's knowledge or consent. What bothers me about this is that if your 13-year-old daughter who can legally keep a parent in the dark does get pregnant, who is responsible? Well, it is pretty obvious that at age 13 you are a minor, who is too young to work, drive, enter into a legal contract or manage a child. The state says you can't do these things because of your age, yet when it comes to a decision that could devastate a Childs life like sex; they have all the rights in the world. Therefore, the child is either given up for adoption, aborted, neglected or the parents have to take on the responsibility for the child. If the parents now have to take on the responsibility for an irresponsible act performed by a minor, then why are they not allowed to be present and have some say during a sex related conversation with the doctor?

Here is another example: You have a severely disabled child whom is an incompetent party. They know nothing about sex and can't learn because of their disability, but they have the right to have sex and get pregnant. Guess who takes on the responsibility for this? The parent who had no says in the matter to begin with or the taxpayers. Is this logical or fair? No, it is not. However, to suggest a vasectomy, sterilization or a birth control shot or IUD would be labeled as fascist philosophy. If the Nazi party never came to power, I think any of these solutions would seem logical and the responsible thing to do. However, we are cursed by the Nazi legacy, which makes logical humane ideas look like fascism.

Chapter 12

Crime

There are 8-17 year old kids raping, robbing and murdering people. What is most unsettling about this is that sometimes they laugh about it. These children are taught no morals, or values. This is all just sick entertainment for them! There is certainly no remorse! Many are the result of an unwanted pregnancy and many don't even know who the father is? Many of their fathers who were just like them are dead, in prison or left long before they were born. Many of the mothers are more concerned about their next fix than teaching morals and values.

They have section 8 housing, government checks, food stamps and food banks to provide their basic needs. If they want more they just steal it from someone else, then kill them for fun. It's a laugh riot! They dominate and intimidate their way through life and end up in prison or dead. But in their wake they are sure to leave behind many more just like them! Some go to public schools, but not for an education, but for the opportunity to sell drugs, steal, rape and rob. Regardless they strain the system to the max. If you call it what it is, then you are a politically incorrect racist. This crime needs to be punished harshly! Not just a slap on the wrist! Murders should be sentenced to death if they are convicted without a doubt or sentenced to hard labor! No sitting around the prison exercising and eating or raping, beating and intimidating the new arrivals and organizing gang activities, but spending time in hard labor and paying back society for the privileges of freedom and the government checks they abused!

America is becoming a soulless society. Kids today are into superficiality and materialism. They are raised with so-called reality television, which portrays a warped way of life. Every other word is bleeped out from the soulless foul mouth stars of the show. The basis for these shows seems to be sex, materialism and parties with an emphasis on having a really bad attitude. Fighting and pushing the envelope to higher and higher forms of rudeness, vulgarity and sexual promiscuity seems to be the trend. Paris Hilton is a great example of the superficiality in American; she is famous for absolutely nothing, but being a rich bitch. That's what people idolize these days. She parties and spends money. That is all there is to her, but that is all there is to many young people today. There is very little faith in anything higher than them, and they have no respect for themselves or anybody else.

It is sad to walk down the street and say hi to a passing teenager who will not even acknowledge you, because they have no manors or sense of respect. Even more unsettling is that they have no sense of right or wrong. But, how can you without faith? The atheist of the world is on a quest like the old religious crusaders. They are hell bent on removing anything that has to do with faith and god for some reason? To me this really does not make sense? What will they achieve in the end, a lawless world of anarchy? That is the only result that can come from it. And why do they even care if they feel we are all just an accident anyway? If I were them I would be trying to have as much fun as possible before they slip into the abyss of nothingness instead of wasting my valuable days on removing god.

Let's face it! God or no god, society cannot exist without faith. Having a belief in something is what keeps people accountable. If people feel that just maybe there is a higher power that knows you're every thought, then people are less likely to do horrible things. Faith is what keeps you from stealing when there is no one around and no way of getting caught. Some people believe in karma. They think that what comes around goes around. This is a type of spiritual accountability, but many people nowadays believe that when they are alone in their room, there is nothing there, but them. What a lonely, depressing existence! I really think this is why many teenagers are so depressed. They are looking for something, but have been taught that there is nothing there.

Even as a small child I believed in something without being told to. Every culture in the world has had some sort of faith in their history. A mustard seed of faith is all you need to stay accountable and to feel that there is a purpose. Without faith nothing really matters. No matter what you accomplish in the end it amounts to nothing and that is a depressing thought for anybody. However, a lot of people don't want accountability, because they are selfish and want to do what they want to do without guilt. But faith brings happiness, accountability, morals, kindness and love. These are things that people should not be trying to get rid of, but get more of. In the end it will be a happier world.

A good example of what a faithless society has brought us is the inner city gangsters. They are fatherless, foul, cruel, vulgar, rude, and loud, void of kindness or love. They rape, rob, pollute and murder without conscious. They spit out kid after kid who will end up just like them. There is nothing and as a result they are nothing. They intimidate and harass and cause nothing but pain and grief. Even when you can't see them they leave signs of themselves by polluting their ugly name throughout the city. They are a cancer that must be stopped! Unfortunately they are the ones who are idolized by today's teens, because they are accountable to nobody and do as they please, but what an ugly, ugly world they leave behind, and in reality I really don't think people, even teens want their insecure world of terror and uncertainty!

In many countries the sentence for drunk driving is death; this sounds harsh, but guess what, there are almost no drunk drivers. For theft they cut off a hand or two. And guess what, there is little to no crime! We have serial killers lounging away in U.S. Prisons; eating, exercising, reading and using up the taxpayers money. They negotiate deals to preserve themselves. These are people that murder innocent people for their personal pleasure with no thought of the suffering they brought to the victims or their families. To add insult to injury they callously describe in morbid detail how they ended those innocent lives, some even laugh about it! They are sociopaths whom are concerned only for themselves. They buy time and luxuries by agreeing to tell about a few more victims they have slain. When they have already admitted to and it has been proven through DNA and other means that they without a doubt are already guilty to many murders. There should be a no tolerance policy, not one; two, three strikes you're out! If you are convicted of first degree premeditated murder you should be done away with 30 days after conviction or sooner.

I am not talking about someone who killed someone in self-defense or defending his or her family or an innocent victim or by accident or the wife or child who has been force raped and beaten for years. I am talking about hardcore killers who kill innocent victims for their sick personal pleasure and gain! Including the 13 year old who has just shot a few people deliberately and is laughing his cocky head off about it. He is accountable! If the penalties are strict, most people will think before acting. I mean these crimes are the ones that have to be proven beyond a shadow of a doubt. Otherwise there could be some very unfortunate circumstances.

German chancellor Angela Merkel in 2008 wanted tougher penalties for juveniles who commit violent crimes. In Germanys 2008, statistics juveniles preformed 43 percent of all violent crimes, half of which were immigrants. That is a large number considering as of 2004 statistics the immigrant population in Germany was roughly only 12%. This paints a pretty clear picture. 12% of the population committing half of the Juvenal crimes! In the past most Juvenal offenders got away with probation. Seeing that this had little effect and seeing repeat offenders, Merkel wanted incarceration time and or a boot camp program. I agree with both. In this way the criminals will feel the pain of the crime they committed and the boot camp will hopefully help educate and improve attitudes which in effect should reduce repeat offenders! Also, in her plan she wanted to be able to deport immigrants easier after such offences!

This is a good plan in my opinion and needs to be carried out. However, some think it is unfair and cruel and are fighting against it. That is exactly why we have such a high rate of crime. People are not punished severely enough for it! The harsher the punishment the less likely there will be offenders. Yes, I agree that treatment should be humane and fit the crime, but the punishment needs to be hard enough to change actions and attitudes! Immigrants who live in another country should be especially courteous since they are the guests! However, in reality they are, as statistics show especially discourteous! Therefore, I don't feel a bit sorry for their deportation!

Attitudes would be a lot different if some **morals and values** were taught in public schools, but again that would take us back to the political correctness issue. We wouldn't want to be politically in correct! Some atheists who believe in nothing anyway go out of their way to have laws passed to take the 10 commandments out of our schools and anything to do with god. They are highly offended by this. If everything is nothing to them anyway why do they even care? Do they want a lack of values and morals in society? If you don't believe in anything then there is nothing to say that murdering, stealing, torturing or raping someone is bad. What are the Ten Commandments anyway? Thou shall not steal? Are they saying that they want it to be all right to steal? Thou shall not kill. Is this offensive? Do they think it is ok to kill? Most of the Ten Commandments are good basic rules for life regardless of what you believe in! Call them something else if you don't want them to be associated with a certain religion, but by all means teach morality in our schools!!!

A juvenile who does not have a good two parent family, which teaches them values, morals and fair play is where the problem starts. The crack whore who gets pregnant produces a child with very little chance. There are always exceptions to this rule, but in general these irresponsible parents are guilty of a heinous crime! Or at least it should be a crime! Because the net result of this irresponsibility has long reaching consequences for society!

The child or children she produces in most cases will end up in the system; which is far from perfect! These children will probably follow in their parent's footsteps with welfare, crime and a total lack of concern for anybody, because of a lack of morals. They can't have morals if someone does not teach them. So, many of the world's problems start with the parents Parenthood should be planned and the children should be taught morals and values. Our world is just over flowing with bad parents and as a result everyone suffers! I look at some kids today and there is a void. They have not been taught to have a conscious!

The problems associated with bad parenting range from crime all the way to a national deficit. The taxpayers are paying for the welfare checks these irresponsible people receive and also the police force that has to deal with them and the prison and legal system that has to prosecute and incarcerate them! These are huge expenses that are almost all the result of bad parenting and un-planned parenthood. We all know that some bad parents produce good kids and good parents can have bad kids, but those are just the exceptions that people just like to argue over.

The majority of our problems are cause from a flawed system, which in effect results in bad parents who produce bad kids that we all have to pay for! Attitude is hard to change. However, the first step to a happier, healthier and cleaner world is to stop irresponsible parents from having children. EVERY child at the age of puberty should have an IUD or other birth control implement. This will eliminate accidental pregnancy among teens.

When the child reaches adulthood and has the resources, education and desire to start a family. Then the IUD can be removed by a health care professional after their qualifications are reviewed. They should also be married or have a mate who also has the willingness and desire to care for children. They also need to be drug free as to help reduce the risks of birth defects and to be stable parents. People with drug addictions are not stable, dependable people. Mental illness and criminal involvement should also be factors. Not misdemeanors in the past or an offense here and there, but a pattern of life long criminal activity should be reviewed.

I have often heard people complain that you need a license for everything, but you need no license or qualifications whatsoever for the most important job there is, and that is being a parent! People will argue how requiring a license would impose on freedoms, but our freedoms are imposed on all the time regarding lessor issues. All laws, rules and regulations prevent the freedom to do as we please, so why is it so much different to add a parenting license?

Chapter 13

Happiness

One evening I saw an interesting program on the happiest and un-happiest countries on earth. Interestingly enough the global study showed that Denmark was rated as the happiest place on earth and not Disneyland! One would think it would be someplace tropical and warm and not a place like Denmark where the citizens are taxed on 68% of their income and it can be downright cold and gloomy in the winter? Why is this? Well, the majority (91%) of Denmark's population of just fewer than 5.5 million is of Danish decent. Of the remaining 8.9% who are immigrants or descendants from recent immigrants, come from South Asia or the Middle East, Iceland and Faroese. So, there is not an overload of immigrants and they actually have immigration laws to keep the level down.

The most recent immigration law passed in 2001 came after an influx of immigrants from the Arab world. To me this is understandable, since Arabic nations are known for their radical religious beliefs and terrorism. I am not trying to stereotype all Arabs and I DO believe in freedom of religion. However, when your religions spill over into innocent peoples life's through acts of terror then there is cause for concern when you are part of that group! Call it racial profiling if you will, but it is what it is! Even if you are not a fanatic and disagree with terrorism, people can't help forming a stereotype! That is just the way it is! Even if you don't want to be prejudice, it can be very hard when certain groups of people consistently do certain things. As I said before the few can ruin it for the many. Again this seems politically incorrect by the standards of most Nations But, I understand Denmark wanting to safeguard their happy community against this! The government will not even allow the women to cover their faces. This has also caused controversy. However, the Danes want to see your face and know who you are. Criminals wear masks to hide their identity. Why should ordinary citizens hide who they are? If these are Denmark's rules, then follow them, or go back to your own country and wear your mask there!

The birth rate is low, but not so low that the population is not stable. The birth rate is 1.74 children per woman, but the population is still averaging a small growth rate of 0.33%. The Kingdom of Denmark is a constitutional monarchy and it is required that all education be free. This includes secondary and above and health care is provided for everybody! Although the taxes are high the people are without wants and don't feel deprived of anything! With a strong close knit community of people of a similar making and of people who think alike and share the same values comes happiness!

This political system would be abused in other countries. However, the Danish people are not selfish. They know that if the overall population is happy then the individual will be happy. Even social groups and activities are promoted and subsidized by the government. The people have more value in community than they do in material possessions as in other industrialized countries! The Danes are very health and environmentally conscious! Although everyone can afford a car most chose to ride a bike instead. Not only does it keep people fit, but also it keeps the air clean and reduces traffic and the bikes are also free for anybody to use!

The countries that were found to be the un-happiest were usually countries that had corrupt governments. Italy was noted as the un-happiest country in Europe because of the crime and corruption.

Other countries that were ranked as some of the un-happiest in the world included many African nations such as Zimbabwe, Uganda, Kenya and Somalia who are ravaged by Aids, starvation, corrupt governments and on-going wars! Iraq was also listed as one of the un-happiest places on earth with its on-going terrorism.

You usually find un-happiness in countries and communities that cannot trust their government or who really have no government to speak of? I mentioned earlier that countries like Somalia are countries in name only and who have no real government other than the warlords who ravage the county and its citizens! There is a tremendous amount of insecurity and fear in countries like this! How can you be happy if you are in constant danger?

How can you be happy if you don't know where your next meal will come from or if you are ravaged by disease and have no hospitals or health care? Even the volunteer groups that try to go in and help these people are victims of gangs and warlords who steal the food and medical supplies that are brought in for the poor. Much of it is stolen and used to feed the warlords and their gangs or sold for cash to buy arms, so they can continue the never-ending senseless violence. These are selfish aims, but when the goals are unselfish and are for everyone's health and happiness like in Denmark, the results are obvious!

The happiest countries were found to have a government that was not corrupt and actively worked for the people. Singapore was listed as the happiest country in Asia However; they also have some of the strictest laws. But, because of these laws and because of a fair government and social programs the crime rate is very low and people are very happy. Government officials are also highly paid to keep them from resisting the urge for corruption. People know the laws are strict, but have no desire to break them, so it is not a concern! There are some countries that don't have great social programs and extreme poverty, but the people are still happy. Places in India are an example. The reason they found for their happiness was because of the strong community and bond they had with one another and religion.

That brings us to the United States. The lone super power and wealthiest country on earth! How happy are the Americans? Well, they only ranked 23rd in this study. That is a pretty low ranking for the wealthiest country on earth! Why are we not happier? I have a few theories? For one we are choking on our liberties. We have more freedom than I believe is healthy. Our crime rate is far higher than most industrialized nations. Several years ago I read some statistics on gun related violence and back then in the early 90's there was something like 10,000 gun related murders in the U.S. Annually. In other countries, like England and Japan the numbers were only a handful. We have everything money can buy, but we are bored. Our constitution even has the term "the pursuit of happiness" But happiness is not something you can pursue!

Happiness is a by-product of other things. The more you pursue it, the more you will miss the mark! It is this ongoing struggle to get enough to make us happy that ultimately leads to un-happiness! We will do anything moral or immoral to get that last piece of the happiness puzzle. This kind of drive towards happiness is what creates greed, jealousy, un-organized and organized crime, corporate corruption, employee corruption, police corruption, and government corruption!

I see this country being destroyed by greed, and urban sprawl is swallowing our beautiful natural environment and replacing it with housing developments and homes so generic and packed in so tight it is sickening, strip malls galore with little or no personality. You can't tell one town from the next. It is just a blur of traffic, Wal-Marts,

Targets, Fred Meyers, McDonalds and smog! The trees that turn carbon dioxide into fresh oxygen are being clear-cut in huge swaths. When I was a kid I actually lived in a sub-division that had trees. Now they will not leave one out of a whole forest. It is easier and more profitable to just take them all down and after all developers are in the business of profit! Besides, if you leave a tree it might fall on the house and get pine needles on the roof. Such an inconvenience and liability, right? In my old neighborhood filled with trees, I never had a single one fall on my house! Some neighbors did, but very few over many years. It is worth the risk and extra maintenance to keep some trees! Developers and logging companies are even putting pressure on our National Forests and public lands.

They want to open them up to logging, mining and development. The Giant Redwoods, some of which have been around long before the birth of Christ were barely saved! Loggers would have had no concern about cutting down each and every one of these beauties for a buck. Money that would have been spent in short time! And the wooden structures built with the material would have been rotten and gone in a hundred or so years. Open spaces that are supposed to be preserved for future generations and for all time.

At least we have some regulations though, because in South America they are logging something like 17 square miles per day of rain forest and not re-planting. Every year a forest the size of the state of Wyoming disappears forever. You don't have to be a mathematician to figure out that we are screwed in a very short time if this continues, but it does continue. How this is even legal is a mystery? These forests affect the entire world and the global community should band together and not allow this destruction to continue!

And it is all because of greed and over population! The developer, businessman, politician, and corporations can't take enough fast enough to satisfy their greed! A businessman will argue that if you're not growing your dying! In reality it is exactly the opposite! Some of our most brilliant minds are working every day to find new, faster, more efficient ways to keep up with the population growth and the insatiable desire for more. They use all the technology available to extract, refine and stretch the earth's resources to the limit when the answer is so simple. Balance!

Balance of population leads to a balance of resources and a healthy environment. We need to protect the environment and everything in it. We are so politically correct on something's, but somehow feel we have the right as humans to take and destroy anything we want, since there is nothing or no one of higher intelligence to tell us otherwise. We have laws to protect minors and incompetent parties who can't protect themselves, but don't give other living organisms any right of survival.

Chapter 14

Morals

Morals, values and faith are major fundamentals that are seriously lacking in our society. Atheists are busting their asses to do away with religion. Not understanding that without faith there is only superficiality. They want so badly to do away with the Ten Commandments. Ten basic rules that everyone should live by religious or not! Without a belief system there is no reason not to do what you want as long as you can get away with it, right? It is OK to steal murder and commit adultery as long as you don't get caught, right? Why not? If you take God out of the picture and the Ten Commandments from our schools then that nagging little angel on your shoulder won't be upsetting your conscious, right? Some cultures that are not particularly religious still have a belief system that makes them think about the good of others before themselves. That is why Denmark is happy!

The people and the government are not thinking about personal gain as much, but for the greater good of the community! Thinking about others or a higher power above you is what makes happiness! Community and caring is what makes happiness! Selfishness, greed, sex and material possessions will not make you happy! America is a good example of that! Our kids have everything, but are bored! They don't get the exercise and the adventure they need, they sit around texting, emailing, I-poding, watching TV, playing video games and eating McDonalds. There is not enough family time playing board games, playing outdoors with our kids or in prayer with one another! Take your kids rock climbing, skiing, swimming, biking, camping or something that ads, excitement, exercise and adventure to their life! Going to the movies and watching others live their life is not enough!

Our spouses are disposable. If things get rocky, just get out of the marriage and find someone who sees eye to eye with you, agrees with your views and makes you happy, right? Ultimately you will see flaws in the next one and the next one. It is a vicious cycle! The divorce rate is now pushing 60% in The U.S. There is not a strong sense of family or community. Morals are almost totally absent! That is why kids in the hood have no problem shooting and beating each other or anyone who happens to cross their path! Most were not introduced to anything but drugs, sex and violence. This crime is how they entertain themselves, because they are bored. There are too many of them with too much time on their hands and no faith, goals, father figures or a strong community to help them see it any other way.

Some middle class kids don't care about anything, but gadgets and the newest stuff they can get from their parents, whom for some kids are nothing more to them than an ATM machine to provide them with trinkets for their amusement, and a chauffeur service. There are not enough family time or family values instilled in them. Far too many American children are fat, spoiled and rude! And it is the parents and our society that are to blame. When children are born they are like a piece of clay, and it is up to the sculpture (parents & society) how they want to sculpt them? They must be taught to have self-esteem, responsibility, morals, work ethic, and manners and be introduced to healthy eating and exercise habits. We are reaping what we sow.

Countries like Denmark are happy because they care not only about community, but also about the environment, architecture, the arts, and history. You see buildings that are century's old, amazing architecture that is proudly preserved and a valuable link to the past, cute sidewalk cafes, museums and a culture that is over a thousand years old. You see a culture and a race that probably looks much the same as they did when they were Vikings. You won't see a lot of racial mixing or washing away of their Scandinavian blood.

You won't see litter and filth like you do in some other countries, because they have pride in where they live and a concern of how what they do affects others. You won't see gangs and drive byes, because they have no desire in hurting one another or disturbing the peace. Shootings, robbing and raping are nearly non-existent. You won't see rude behavior or foal language much and you won't see corrupt politicians or business practices! Countries like this look at the greater good, because they know that when the community benefits, so does the individual! These of course are generalizations, and I by no means intend to say that bad behaviors do not exist here, but far less than in many countries!

America does not have a country like this. Although, you have many caring individuals, you also have the scum of the earth and everywhere in between. It is hard to have a balance of values with the tremendous diversity and size of the U.S. Here you have a melting pot of different races, religions, cultures and ideologies and they don't always mesh very well together. Having this kind of diversity is one of the reasons the U.S. is successful, but also one of its down falls! There are U.S. citizens that don't believe in anything the constitution stands for. There are illegal aliens and citizens who benefit from the U.S. But do not give anything back. In fact they work hard to undermine the U.S. from within. Illegal aliens certainly don't pay any income taxes, but they manage to reap the benefits of the taxpayers. Because of the freedom the U.S. offers to everyone we are literally sleeping with our enemies! Many radical Muslims call the U.S. Home. Atheists want to do away with any mention of God and Christian based holidays such as Christmas and Easter. These are cherished traditions for many Americans. Many protest against Christian symbols like Christmas trees. These are traditions our country has grown up with, but now with the growing diversity many want to take away the good things that most of us know and love. It is like some people are going out of their way to destroy the country from within and make this country ugly.

Many people have no consideration for other people, animals or the beauty of this country, people throw garbage all over our parks, streets and open spaces and they have no pride, responsibility or uniform values. I took a month long trip to New Zealand once and was amazed at how clean it was! In America you see garbage and litter strewn all over the sides of the freeways, but this is very rare in New Zealand. I probably only saw a couple of cigarette butts on the ground over the entire month and I was all over the South island and a small part of the North.

It is a disgrace, but people don't seem to care in America for some reason if they have to look at junk all the time? It takes the same amount of time to throw their garage away in the proper receptacles as it does to throw it onto the streets. The only thing I can figure is that they do it just to be rude or they are just lazy? Americans are notorious for being rude and selfish. New Zealand takes pride in the cleanliness of their country and we should too! However, this is hard when Americans are raised to be rude or are the result of irresponsible parents who teach them nothing and a government that allows them everything. Including free speech, which has become a joke and a polluted distortion of what our fore fathers, intended it to be. Rappers exercise their free speech all the time with lyrics about killing, robbing and raping. I don't think this is what our fore fathers had in mind?

The United States is still probably the best country to live in, but just because of that fact it does not mean that it will always be that way and that we shouldn't look at the finer qualities of countries like, Denmark, Sweden, Germany, New Zealand and many others as examples! They may not be as rich, but a high standard of living is not necessarily better than a great quality of life and both can be managed with some work!

I think we need to be careful about allowing so many immigrants into our country. Most politicians acquiesce to the immigration problem and offer solutions like amnesty and ID cards. I disagree! I think every illegal immigrant should be deported! They are **illegal!** They are not from this country and have no business being here. The benefits to living in the U.S. are great, so to reap those benefits they need to go through the process of doing it legally! And I don't agree that we should just make it easier for them! If anything we should make it challenging enough so that the immigrants that make it are of the best quality, proficient in the language and the most determined! This will weed out the losers and criminals.

The argument with deporting all illegal aliens is that there are just too many and many have been here so long that they have established roots. This sounds cold, especially when you would be separating families or deporting parts of a family that were born after the illegal entry, but the offenders and parents should have thought of that before they entered the country illegally! But, that is precisely the goal for many illegals. They want to establish roots and have children born on U. S. Soil, so you can't get rid of them. Most believe that the job is too big! Well, it does not have to be done in a day, but sooner or later they will show up somewhere and that's when you deport them. If the feeling is that there are too many to round up then that says right there that our border security and penalties are way too soft! I do think the consequences should be harsh. Not because I think that people should suffer, but because it is our very softness that has caused this problem!

The United States could make a deal with Mexico to help them organize and industrialize to provide jobs in their own country and boost the economy on a larger scale than what we are currently doing. We could be better trade partners as well. However, there would have to be strict policies to avoid government corruption, which Mexico is notorious for. The United States would need to implement stricter measures to monitor this.

The United States definitely needs to crack way down on the criminal activity that undermines the security and confidence of this country. If people don't feel safe and secure they will never obtain the happiness Denmark has. The legal system needs a major makeover to help address this too. Some attorneys are experts at trickery and deception; painting known criminals in a good light to get them free and back on the streets.

They are only concerned for the win any way they can get it! Many have no problems with lying, deception, Manipulation, intimidation, coercion and trickery! And they are paid to do so. They are paid to win, but that does not make what some of them do morally right? Our laws need to be strict enough to keep people from offending. Singapore has very strict laws, but that does not keep them from being happy! The knowledge that they have security and order is probably a major factor in their happiness?

Chapter 15

Immigration

Immigration has been a major source of frustration and controversy in the EU and North America. This is a continuing debate among conservatives, moderates and liberals. Some are of the opinion that there are too many immigrants flooding into the EU and North America. A recent study in Germany by a national working on youth violence said that every third school age child in the study agreed that there were far too many foreigners in Germany; another third said they pretty much agreed. This study was done at a time when Germany was pushing the EU to take in more Iraqi Christian refugees. The conclusion was that xenophobia is still rampant among German youths.

I am myself a Christian and I am not unsympathetic to the immigrants struggle. However, if you let one in, then it would be unfair to not let them all in. But if you let them all in, then the race, economy, culture and identity of Germans will disappear. That is what many in Germany are probably afraid of? Not to mention other social factors such as the increase in crime, more competition for jobs and the cultural differences that affect the lifestyles and values of Germans. If people show a concern over immigration, the first thought is not why, or how, can we address these concerns, but rather it is dismissed as xenophobia and the people that express their concerns are seen as intolerant.

The fact of the matter is that there are huge numbers of people in need of help! There are so many, that the numbers would swallow the EU and North America. I do sympathize with their struggles. They are persecuted in their country because of their faith, they live under corrupt governments or they are suffering from disease and poverty. It is perfectly understandable that they would want to come to a better and more prosperous country and I don't blame them for that. However, the concerns of the nation's people regarding crime, pollution, and loss of race, culture and identity should not simply be dismissed as xenophobia! These are real and valid concerns. In East Germany many authentic Germans say there are more immigrants than Germans, and the problem is that if you drown out the host countries population, then the authentic Germans become the minority, and the majority usually rules. What it really becomes is a non-hostile takeover. Before long the culture becomes something other than a German-Christian culture.

The majority will bring their cultural ideas and race into the mix turning it into the same place they escaped. When going to Germany or any other EU country, instead of seeing the authentic peoples from those lands you will see a majority of other races and cultures. You will and do see headscarf's and people wearing Burke's from the Arabic nations more than Germans, Indian cultures more than Germans, Asians and Buddhists. You might try to find an authentic German café, but instead all you find is authentic Arabic, Asian and Indian foods. Some different cultures are OK and should not be discriminated against. It is nice to have some variety, but I don't think it is OK at all to go so far. Limits should be imposed!

Even when the white Irish immigrants became such a problem in New York during the mid-19th century, restrictions were imposed limiting the amount allowed into the country. The five points in New York started to become a gangland and the continuing flood of immigrants from Ireland began to become a real burden on the Irish immigrants who had long been established. Once limits were enforced the quality of life and standard of living improved drastically!

So this is not about the color of someone's skin, country of origin or religious affiliation. It is about quality of life and standard of living. A liberal's response to this would be that all are entitled to the same quality of life and standard of living. I wish it worked that way, but land and resources are limited and it simply cannot work. If we let immigrants enter first world countries in unlimited amounts the quality of life and standard of living will increase for the immigrants, for a time, but decrease for the host people of the host country. Eventually with unbridled immigrant procreation the quality of life and standard of living will diminish for everyone, including the immigrants. The mass exodus from Ireland during the 19th century is evidence of that.

When immigrant populations swelled as it did during that time the inevitable result becomes greater competition for jobs and resources. The result becomes crime and pollution, starvation and disease. These are things no one wants! You would have to be crazy to want these things! But, that is exactly what you will get with a tolerant attitude. People are trying to help and make the world a better place, and I understand that! But, the end result will be exactly the opposite! The world will become a worse place for everyone!

If there was some basic common sense and foresight anyone could see that. This open arms policy is delusional! I am not for saying screw the rest of the world and its people, but the peoples from these nations must take on the responsibility for themselves. I am not against immigration, but there needs to be stricter policies and to allow only the immigrants who are of the best quality. Not just anyone. Again I go back to the solution, which is for these people not to have so many kids. Have an amount that you can provide for. If people were more responsible in this regard they would have a greater quality of life and standard of living! If you are from a starving third world county, why are you having 10 kids? They certainly will not be given the life they deserve! The solution is to drag them all to a country that will take care of them, and that is why people have a problem with some immigrants and the leniency some governments show them!

If people want to help these people then they need to help them make their country a better place, instead of bringing them home and making their own country a worse place!

This all sounds good in theory, but what about places like Somalia? Advance countries tried to help them for years only to be shot at, murdered, beaten and robbed as a thank you! Eventually the U.S. Gave up on Somalia and declared it a failed state The concern is that even though there is tremendous violence in countries like Somalia, there are also good people in need of help! What do you do about them? Do you just leave them behind? Well, this has to be looked at realistically. What are the options? Some say help as many as you can, by adopting or allowing them to immigrate into your country. I can understand this, but what about the vast majority you can't help? Moreover, some of the ones you do help by bringing them into the fold create the same problems in your own country that you are trying to spare them from in theirs; adding their problems to yours. It is no different than the old lady that collects every stray cat she can find or the good people who allow down and out friends or strangers to stay in their home.

My brother is the most giving Christian man I know, and he would take in anyone in need, only to be used and stolen from. This was not always the case, but a person and a country need to be discerning. You need to ask yourself: Am

I endangering my family by allowing this down and out stranger to live in my house? Am I endangering my country by allowing these immigrants to enter my country?

I know a lot of people that just want to do their little bit in this out of control world. I think that is commendable. It makes them feel better about themselves and is a legitimate help to the ones they help. I do not discourage this one bit, but again we must be very discerning, so that we protect children, our countries and ourselves. Helping can potentially hurt more than it helps! There have been examples of people taking in the homeless and being robbed, raped and murdered.

I was watching the evening news and heard a report of a man that allowed a homeless man to live in his home with his wife and children. He also found odd jobs for the man to help him financially. This went on for several weeks or more. When, one day this homeless man kidnapped the generous man's wife and stole his van. He drove his victim halfway across the state. Eventually she escaped or was released and returned home safely to her husband, but the outcome could have been very different! It was an unwise choice on the generous man's part. He risked the life of his family trying to do the right thing. How would it feel to know, you let a complete stranger into your house and later find out that he had sexually molested your child? I have no doubt that there are many people out there that know exactly how it feels!

Of course someone in your own family could molest your child. Not all situations are avoidable. As a parent you simply have to make the best possible choices to protect your family and be responsible; the same also holds true for a nation.

Even though dangers exists with-in a nation, that nation needs to be responsible and discerning when it comes to immigration, and to not add to the already existing internal issues. There are ways of helping people without endangering your family or a nation. The sad fact is that not everyone can be helped. That does not mean we shouldn't try? Not necessarily, but I do not think that it is possible to cure every terrorist from his or her murderous convictions or every criminal from theirs! There are mentally ill people out there that cannot or do not want to be cured. There are radical extremists who have had flawed ideology forced upon them from birth. In those cases there may be no other choice than to distance ourselves from them, but first making sure that they do not have the ability to hurt us.

We need to ban foreigners from hostile countries from entering our country. If any are allowed in, they should be screened thoroughly. Middle Eastern terrorist organizations don't really have the capability to hurt us here. The only reasons soldiers are dying there is because they are with-in the limited range of rocket propelled grenades, AK-47"s and IED's. The only way they can hurt us here is by entering our country, and this should not be allowed. This will be labeled politically incorrect because it will be looked at as stereotyping all Middle Easterners. This attitude needs to stop, because it is very difficult to know who is good from the Middle East and who is bad. Another decision, which is viewed as politically incorrect by today's standards, was the Japanese internment camps. But, in those days we were in a war where the existence of our country and freedom was at stake and they did not take any chances back then; now days we don't see it that way. Newt Gingrich thinks that the U.S. will have to lose a major city before we wake up, and it is only a matter of time before we do.

Iran is frantically working to develop a nuclear weapon and the world knows it, but no one wants to risk doing anything about it other than forcing trade embargos and issuing warnings. People don't want war and conflict. Countries just sit back watch and hope that things will be all right. They issue warnings, but Iran is a country that without a doubt once a nuclear device is obtained, will launce it strait at Israel. No one wanted to confront Hitler either, but they could have saved 55 million lives had they stopped the beast before it was fully-grown. In the case of Hitler the Allied nations were not sure how far he would go? They thought if they just gave him a little more he would be satisfied? But, with Iran their intentions have been made perfectly clear. They want to wipe Israel off the map, and if they can, destroy the U.S. Too.

The Iranians fully expect a retaliatory strike and want to be destroyed themselves as to fulfill their destiny. When they launce that first missile then all of the sudden the internment of Middle Easterners will no longer be looked at as politically incorrect. No one will oppose a retaliatory strike either. All U.S. citizens will be all for closing down our borders to foreigners from hostile nations, even the far left liberals. Unfortunately, the time to stop it before it starts will have past. We know what happened in the late 1930's when the English Prime Minister Neville Chamberlain tried to appease Hitler. It did not work then when the world had suspicions about Hitler and now that we know the clear intentions of Iran the world is still trying the historically failed strategy of appeasement.

The Allied nations swore that they would learn from that mistake and would never repeat it, but here we are again over 75 years later making the same mistakes. What we need to do is walk into that country with everything we have and dismantle Iran's nuclear program before it's too late. We also need to completely disarm the Middle East and close our borders to Middle Easterners with very limited and special exceptions. We need to boycott Middle Eastern Oil and send them back to the Stone Age.

We need to change to alternate sources of energy. It is a huge task. But, if we knew for a fact that if we did not change our ways the human race would become extinct with-in a half century or less, you bet your ass we would figure it out real quick! The technology already exists, but it is not being implemented on a full scale, because of greed. Greed and power are worthless and narrow-minded goals when the human race is on the verge of extinction! I am amazed at how advanced we are, yet how primitive our thinking is when it comes to basic common sense issues.

Chapter 16

GREED

There are, give or take approximately 358 to 1426 billionaires in the world at the time of this writing, and their combined assets exceed the total annual income of the world's 2.3 billion poorest people. This is roughly, 45% of the total global population. The top 20% of the world's people receive nearly 83% of the world's total income and the poorest 20% receive only 1.4%, a ratio of 60 to 1. Something is really wrong with this figure!

One thing this statistic shows is that greed outweighs the masses. Yes, we could convert from fossil fueled commuter cars to hydrogen or electric powered cars. However, the reason this does not happen is because of greed! The oil companies are not going to lay down their riches for the masses or the environment.

Greedy lending institutions fueled the housing crises, which began with the boom in 2003 and declined into disaster with the bankruptcy of many of the largest banks in the world in September 2008. This boom also benefited greedy developers as more and more people could afford to get into housing with the new 0 down, 80-20, interest only adjustable rate mortgages. Loans that people with credit scores as low as 580 could qualify for. As a result people, who could not buy homes before, could now qualify for a mortgage. The result of this was a large supply of buyers and a limited supply of homes. (Supply and demand) This benefited the developers who were building at alarming rates; it benefited the banks that were closing more deals than ever. It also helped everyone else in the housing industry.

The problem was that the prices of homes were going up 20% or more in some areas and nearly everything was selling. Buyers were paying more and more for homes. Not because wages were going up, but because the loans banks were giving were enabling buyers to pay more and more for a home. I was in the industry at the time and immediately saw the problems these loans would eventually cause.

I do not have a PHD in economics from Harvard or Yale, but this was just basic common sense! If I could see it, why couldn't the banks or the buyers? How could the prices go so high when wages were not? It was all about these short term ARMS. I knew something would have to come crashing down, but the financial analysts, CEOs, and the banks denied that we were in a bubble. They were either blinded by the enormous successes they were having or knew that in the end, regardless of what happened to the world economy, that they themselves would rake in billions.

Sure they probably knew that the end result might send the U.S and the world into another great depression and billions of people would suffer as a result, but as far as the individual CEOs were concerned they would become enormously wealthy and escape the crisis on a golden parachute! This is GREED! If the common man could see a problem with all of this, you can bet the CEOs of these large banks knew exactly what was coming!

Five short years later the market came crashing down. As ARM rates went up and up, people could no longer afford their homes and were unable to refinance into a 30 year fixed loan because the qualifying standards got tougher and as a result of late pays due to higher and higher payments, home owners had even worse credit scores. This left one choice. **Sell.** However, others were in the same boat and the market was soon flooded with homes for sale. These homes were now worth less than before and there was negative equity.

All of this resulted in severely damaging the world economy and was all the result of short-term greed. There are now more homes in foreclosure than there has been since the great depression. The consequences of these risky and irresponsible mortgage investments are so severe and far reaching that the culprits should be held accountable. To fix the problem the government stepped in with 700 billion + dollars of the taxpayers' money to bail out these failing banks, our children's children may still have the liability of paying off this debt. Not only should those who benefited not be able to escape with any amount of money they should be imprisoned as an example to the future speculators who would gladly forfeit the world economy and the lives of billions for their personal gain!

How much dam money does one person need anyway? It is wasteful, selfish and enormously cruel to the billions that must suffer. It is this selfish worldly attitude that is destroying this planet and the majority should not stand for it!

The lumber companies are depleting our forests faster than they can be re-grown. In the South American rain forest they are not always replanting and much of the logging is being done illegally. This will destroy our planet and is a result of nothing more than greed. The earth is being stripped for lumber, oil, coal, precious metals and gems to fill the growing demand from a growing population. But, instead of trying to help the world solve problems with resource management and population management, the big companies would rather enjoy the exploding demand for their products. Unfortunately, people can't see beyond their greed and seem to be more concerned for the profit now, than for the future wellbeing of the environment and humanity.

This kind of falls back on my criticism of preaching nothingness as the atheist does! It gives the greedy the, who cares attitude, because nothing matters anyway mentality. This is why I think preaching and teaching atheism is a very dangerous thing in our schools. If you don't know beyond a shadow of a doubt that there is no god, then keep your mouth shut!

All you are doing by teaching atheism to the entire population is forming a nothing matters attitude and that's not good for anyone! Ok, now back to the subject; It is not a lack of know-how or a lack of resources that keeps the rich from solving the world's problems, it is simply that there is a greater desire for the short term and selfish gain, than the desire to help the world. By their estimates, they will be long gone before the collapse of humanity, so who gives a fuck!

As much as it hurts the economy I am glad Lehman Brothers and Bear Stearns who filed bankruptcy in September of 2008 were held accountable and not bailed out by the Government for their irresponsible practices and I hope the CEOs of these companies are not able to escape on their golden parachutes. Although the government or should I say the individual tax payers who are the government are still on the hook for bailing out Fannie Mae, Freddie Mac and AIG at least they are all not totally getting away with it! There are enough great minds on this earth to establish regulations that will protect the average citizen, but also allow the free enterprise system to work. These white collar criminals must be forced see that there is something bigger than themselves, like the over 7 billion people suffering on their behalf and the future generations who will have nothing left for their survival.

One will argue that a surging economy creates millions of jobs that the common person would not have without these greedy men and women and their innovative ideas. I don't disagree with this, but I go back to the main premise of this book, which is balance. A balanced economy will benefit today's population, future generations and the environment our children will have to live in. A balanced population will do the same.

Chapter 17

Obvious problems!

There are some real obvious problems with this world, and one of the more interesting statistics is that at the beginning of the 20th century the population was only 1.6 billion people. But, as we entered the 21st century there was 6.1 billion people, in 2007 we reached 6.6 billion people and in 2011 we have pasted 7 billion people in the world. This is absolutely staggering!

The increase in the human population in the last half-century is absolutely unprecedented! What is even more interesting is that almost all of the growth comes from the less developed countries. Nearly 80 million people are being added each year in the less developed countries. Compare that with the 1.6 million people being added each year in the more developed countries. While the less developed countries keep growing the more developed countries are slowing to a stable population. It is remarkable that the countries that are growing the most are the ones that can afford it the least!

Why is this you ask? Well, the population change has mostly to do with advancements in medicine, economic development, the status of women and other political and technological advancements. The United Nations, church organizations, the Red Cross and other volunteers from industrialized countries go to undeveloped countries and provide medicine, food and water. The intentions are good, but are these benevolent deeds really helping? In some ways yes, but in other ways it is making things worse. The amount of suffering overall is not decreasing, but what the help is doing, is it is enabling less developed countries to increase in population, but not so much in education.

If you look at the level of education in more developed and in less developed countries, you will see that the more educated the people are, the less children they have. In Ethiopia a woman with a secondary education will have only on average 2.2 children, where an Ethiopian woman with no education will have 6.1 children on average. The trend is the same for other developing countries, like Senegal, the Philippines, Honduras and Egypt. Germany has one of the lowest birth rates among industrialized countries at around 1.3 children born per woman. The U.S. has an average of 2.1 children born per woman. The reason the U.S. is higher than Germany is because the U.S. has 20% of the world's immigration, and in the 21st century most of these immigrants are from less developed countries like Mexico and Latin America where it is common to have large families and low education.

The trend is pretty clear, the higher the level of education the fewer children a woman will have. In industrialized countries a woman also has choices. They are more educated and are moving away from traditional gender roles. A woman has the choice of education and the ability to support herself if necessary. In the past European and North American woman were homemakers and bore more children. Now days they have a choice to have children or not. Most women have a motherly instinct and want to have a child or two at some point, but it tends to be later in life and on their terms. Since they are educated they realize what goes into raising healthy children. They think not only of what is required to care for children, but also about college, health care and other things that will benefit their children. An educated woman is not usually going to pump out kid after kid without any thought to how they are going to care for them? Where uneducated women from less developed countries don't think about it, or don't have the basic tools and education to do anything about it. Educated women are fully aware of the various birth control methods. Therefore, they can plan when or if they want to get pregnant?

Therefore, it seems that a lack of education in less developed countries, greed and lack of morals are three of our biggest problems. Other major problems, like the environment, crime and world hunger are directly related. Fix the first three problems and everything else should fall into place! Our number one goal should be education first! Instead of only providing food, water, housing and medicine! If we really want to provide help that will have a lasting effect for all of humanity we must provide at least some basic education to keep these populations from exploding, which in effect puts a larger strain on those trying to provide food, water, housing and medicine to the under privileged.

One would simply wear themselves out trying to feed all these people. The more you help the more help they need, because you are merely enabling a population explosion! The problem just keeps getting bigger and bigger until the industrialized nations helping, either can't feed themselves any longer or have to abandon the ones they use to help in order to keep food on the table for themselves? The result is that the starving people that they began to help are starving again; only there are many times more of them, so the net result of this benevolent act, are far more people suffering! All their hard work will have been in vain. The humane gestures will end up being even more inhumane than if we let nature take its course. If educated industrialized countries are so intelligent, then why are the participants making these basic mistakes?

In the animal world you have rabbits and coyotes. At times the rabbit population is enormous, and as a result the coyotes have plenty to eat. As a natural result the coyote population begins to increase. Over time the rabbit population declines. The more coyotes the more rabbits they eat. Eventually, the coyote's food source gets scarce and the result is that coyotes begin to starve and die out. As the coyotes die out the rabbit population has fewer predators hunting them and then the rabbit population begins to increase once again. This cycle occurs over and over again in the animal kingdom.

Without man's intervention the animal population is dependent on the food resources available. Animal populations go up or down accordingly. However, there should be a difference between humans and animals? Because of the superior intellect of humans, we have the ability to control these cataclysmic up and down, boom and bust cycles if we chose to, and to control our environment. Yet, the same process will happen to us because we do not use our abilities to their full potential. Although, we have been able to change the patterns, in a lot of ways we are not much better at managing than the animals whose populations fluxgate in cycles that are directly dependent on the supply of food, water and habitat.

The only thing we are really doing is prolonging the inevitable. We have done a great job at increasing our crop yields and increasing the amount and quality of the food we grow. We have been very inventive and have found hi-tech mechanized ways of harvesting our crops without as much dependency on manual labor. As a result we are able to grow more with less space, thus freeing up land for subdivisions, strip malls and industry. Through the use of steroids, mechanization and science we have also increased our live stalk yield and our dairy cows are now milked by mechanized machinery and are yielding more milk as a result of hi-tech diets and steroids. Our brilliant minds are focused on producing even more with less. The thinking is that we can continue to grow and grow indefinitely. There is always a creative way to squeeze more out of this earth, but the result in the end will be the same as it is for the rabbit and the coyote. Some of us will die out from lack of resources and I think we are getting close to the precipice of that now. However, it does not have to be this way!

We have already passed our point of sustainability, but we keep trying to squeeze more out of the earth. Experts have already predicted that we will reach zero population growth between 2020 and 2050 with a maximum sustainable capacity of between 6.64 and 7.47 billion people. The population reached 1 billion in 1804, 2 billion in 1927, 3 billion in 1959, 4 billion in 1974, 5 billion in 1986 and 6 billion in 1999. The exponential growth of the human population actual peaked in 1987 and the growth rate has been decreasing every year since. Although the population will continue to increase, it will not do so exponentially.

The reason is resources. Our planet has limited resources. In the back of our minds we all know this, but partly because of greed and other factors we keep trying to squeeze out more and more. One resource that is crucial for survival is fresh drinking water. Only one percent of the world's water is suitable for drinking and it is pretty obvious that the population cannot increase indefinitely. Some might think we can even overcome this issue, by refining seawater. However, doing so requires fuel to run the refineries and other natural resources which are being depleted as well. Therefore this is not the answer either. By prolonging and stretching we are only setting ourselves up for a huge collapse, a collapse that the human race may not be able to recover from. If we would only managed our resources and population this collapse could be avoided, but it does not look like the odds are in our favor. There is some exploration into cleaning up the environment and alternatives to fossil fuel, but it may be too little too late, and the one thing that is being almost totally ignored is getting the less developed countries educated enough to control their birth rates.

The industrialized nations need to provide these less developed countries with a birth control that will work. Not condoms, because, they will just make jewelry out of it! As the population decreases in these areas then the quality of life will go up for everyone in these under developed countries. I am not talking about forced sterilization, because everyone has the right to have children. I am talking about making educated choices and family planning like is done in industrialized countries. This also means controlling our teenage pregnancy in industrialized countries and enforcing birth control among those on welfare.

Chapter 18

WAR

The historical result of dwindling resources has often resulted in WAR. When people start competing for dwindling resources tensions mount and desperation sets in. In today's society we are completely depended on fossil fuel. Nearly everything in the modern age depends on it. We need fuel for transporting ourselves to and from work, we need fuel to transport our food supply from farms around the nation to our local grocery store and even more fuel to transport exotic foods and spices from around the world. We lack nothing in our local grocery stores because of the ability to transport any type of food from anywhere in the world quickly. Everything we use in our everyday life that is made of plastic is also a derivative of fossil fuel.

It is common knowledge that there is not an endless supply of fossil fuel. It took millions of years to create and can't be replenished like the forests can be re-grown. There are creative ways of sucking out previously unobtainable deposits of fuel and more and more deposits will likely be found and extracted. However, this will only prolong the inevitable, not to mention the destruction it will cause our planet. Earth will almost certainly be beyond repair far earlier than the last deposits of oil can be extracted!

Fossil fuel has created a great comfort for the population. We can simply hop on a plane and travel anywhere in the world we want to go, comfortably and in a matter of hours. We have become so dependent on it that as the demand increases and the cost climbs higher the tension and competition will grow. Fossil fuel is something that we will have to have and as the supply dwindles and demand increases the tensions will grow to a point where we will probably take it from those who have it by any means necessary.

First OPEC will be given ultimatums. "Sell us oil at a price we can live with or we will sue you to sell it on our terms!" The pressure will continue until they agree or an excuse is found to just go take it. This will result in an all-out war over oil that has been predicted for generations. Other nuclear powers will not sit idly by while the U.S. or any other nation does this. Everyone is going to want a piece of the pie and like a swarm of locusts every country with the power to take a piece of the pie will descend down on the oil rich countries fighting each other along the way, expediting the decline of the human race!

The lack of fuel will result in famine! Although, there may still be enough food, transporting it will be interrupted because of the scarcity of oil. Parents in their desperation to feed their children and themselves will take food however they can find it. This will undoubtedly result in civil unrest and major violence. Even many of the easy going, good-natured people will resort to their animal instincts to get the necessities for life. After all, this will be for the survival of themselves as well as their loved ones!

Some people will be organized enough to prepare for this day by growing much of their own food and finding alternate forms of transportation, but unfortunately some of those people will be at risk by the unorganized people who instead of pre-planning and problem solving will merely take from others.

Once we eliminate the need for foreign fossil fuel we can simply abandon the tumultuous relationship with the mid-east and let them fight among themselves with their AK-47's, RPG's and IED's. As long as they don't have the ability to reach our allies or us with nuclear intercontinental ballistic missiles, who cares! Once the fuel profits dry up they will not be able to afford a nuclear program anyway and can go back to the way they have been fighting for thousands of years!

These horrible images could be avoided if we act now to educate the undeveloped countries and start making some fairly uncomfortable sacrifices today. The first thing is to educate the poorer countries on birth control and to implement birth control devices that are dependable. The next thing is to eliminate our dependency not only from foreign oil, but also from fossil fuel, period. There may still be a need for fossil fuel in some capacity, but much of our dependency could be greatly reduced prolonging our supply indefinitely. We have been living off the fat of the lamb for such a long time and need to suck it up and start doing things responsibly. The result of our luxuries and excess have only resulted in over populated, overweight, spoiled and depressed societies anyway.

Chapter 19

Transportation

We need reliable, clean public transportation that follows existing arteries, so the option for travel locations is not so limited. These transportation systems should be clean, quiet, spacious and inviting atmospheres where the traveler truly enjoys the experience and are not annoyed by other passengers! The environment needs to be an improvement over the driving environment. You should be able to read, study, watch a movie use a laptop, or PDA. This change of transportation should be a comfort benefit that is looked forward to by the passenger and not a crowded, noisy uncomfortable experience that is dreaded like taking the standard city bus. Commuting on public transportation should be a time of meditation and pleasure!

We need solar, electric, hydrogen or bio-fuels on a limited basis with the lowest emissions possible. We need less urban sprawl and more open space like some European countries have managed. Smaller forms of transportation like scooters or bikes for the independent traveler. With the invention of the computer and especially the Internet many types of jobs can be done from home, eliminating or reducing the need to travel as much.

The new Smart cars in Europe that use diesel get 60 miles per gallon are even better than my motorcycle! I think that using a bio-diesel smart car or a similar vehicle would be even better for conservation and the environment. Although bio-diesel has been affecting food prices, the inedible corn leaves or sugar cane can also be used as a source of fuel. So we have options! I think nuclear energy is very a questionable option, because the nuclear waste cannot be disposed of and must be contained and managed. Ultimately this would spell disaster. Therefore, I don't see this as the best option, unless they find a way of disposing of the waste. Containment is only temporary and we need to be thinking ahead hundreds if not thousands of years. Our future generations should not have to pay for our lifestyle.

We need to go back to using trains to transport food, passengers and supplies instead of using semi-trucks and planes. We will be able to transport more with much less pollution or possibly none? Rural communities could even go so far as to use horse and buggy again. Of course I know this sound ridiculous, but it worked for centuries before, so why not now in some places and in some capacities? Mix some old with some new! We might learn to have some patience again? With the Internet and email, we can and have drastically reduced the need for postal travel. Some methods of travel will be slower than we have become accustom to, but we need to start thinking more of preservation and less of convenience. It is not a bad thing to slow down.

When I was young it was always assumed that we would eventually over populate or destroy this planet through war or the depletion of our recourses. Then people thought that eventually we would have to find another planet to spill our over flowing population onto. Assuming at that time there may be many reachable and habitable planets. Now we know that there are probably not. Mars and possibly some of Saturn or Jupiter's moons are the only viable options and those options would require far more work than managing the one perfect planet we currently live on. Mars is also much smaller than earth and it has not been proven whether or not we could create an atmosphere there that could sustain human life? Our muscles would also become weak and our bones brittle over time without sufficient gravity. I do think if it is possible we should colonize Mars, but only as a back-up planet in the event that something catastrophic should happen to Earth? However, finding another planet to colonize still does not solve the problem. Over time both Earth and Mars would become overpopulated.

Instead of going to such lengths and only for temporary gains, we simply need to implement population control on a humane and global scale! This is the most humane thing we could do! There should not be unwanted pregnancies, teenage pregnancy or welfare recipients with 4, 5, or 12 kids. As I've said before, everyone should have the right to have children and to live a long life regardless of their education, disabilities or income. There should not be extremes, like euthanasia or abortions. There should also not be world hunger! But, the only way we can rid the world of extremes is to manage our population and recourses.

It could be calculated fairly easily as to how many people our planet can sustain given our available and renewable resources. It could be calculated as to how much carbon dioxide is a healthy amount and how much is harmful to the environment. If mathematicians can figure out how many light years it is to Alpha Sentari, then it should be no problem calculating these basic issues? If after calculating how much food, fuel, water, lumber, electricity, etc. we can output that is a safe and renewable, sustainable amount, and then we could determine how large of a population we could sustain indefinitely. If the number is 5 billion, then we need to decrease the birth rate over however many years it takes until we reach that mark and then maintain zero population growth. To maintain the current population every woman needs to have 2.3 children, because some of her offspring will not procreate or die before their child bearing years. Therefore, even if a standard were set for 2 children allowed per woman the population would decrease, and since some women can't or won't have children, other women have the option of more children if they want? At this rate it would take a while to get the population to the proper level, but at least we would be going in the right direction and eventually everyone in the human population would have enough of everything! But, as it is now, eventually things will come to a head and everyone will begin to suffer!

Our goals are so extremely short sided! On Fox I saw a program about the U.S. becoming independent of foreign oil. They mentioned drilling in the Alaskan wilderness where there was an estimated 9 to 16 billion gallons of oil. However, when you look at the broad picture and the amount of oil the U.S. consumes daily, this deposit would last us only 4 months to 2 years and it would take 10 years to extricate the oil and have it ready for use.

Not to mention having a big impact on the environment! There was also mention of drilling in water in the Gulf of Mexico that is over 7,000' deep. This could be done, but what a huge investment in time, money and new technology, just for another short-term gain! These efforts are just buying a little more time, and at the same time undermining the efforts to develop clean and sustainable energy. It may be necessary to explore new possibilities for fossil fuel, but only until we can transition to different modes of transportation and energy.

Chapter 20

Hostile Liberals

As I said earlier, I don't claim to be a conservative or a liberal. As far as the environment I lean towards the left, but in regards to family values, morals and religion I lean to the right. However, since watching the 2008 campaign between Democratic nominees Barack Obama with Joe Biden as his vice presidential pick and Republican nominee John McCain with his VP pick of Sara Palin I am thoroughly shocked and disgusted at how violent the liberals have been! One good example is ABC's morning talk television show the "VIEW" The difference between the way these liberal women (minus Hasslebeck) treat Obama compared to the way they treat McCain is horrendous. They should be downright ashamed of themselves!

Regardless of their views and their political affiliations, they should at least try to show some objectivity and common courtesy toward their guests. They don't have to agree with them and can ask the hard questions, but the shear hatred was rude and unnecessary! They mercilessly snapped at and attacked McCain throughout the entire show. No matter what he said or how calmly he composed himself, they were ruthless. They obviously didn't care what he said or how much sense he made. They weren't listening, they were bullying. Cindy McCain was appalled too as she listened from the back stage! She said, "What are they doing to my husband out there?" If you are objective and a professional you will at least take the time to listen and try to understand where the person is coming from! You don't have to agree, but if you can't listen you will never understand. You learn more from listening than you do from talking, and gain nothing from badgering and harassing! I personally thought that McCain handled it very well by staying professional and to the point unlike his interviewers.

It was quite a contrast when Obama was on their show, they were pawing all over him like school girls and stroking his ego, telling him how handsome he was, as if they were more concerned about his looks, youth and the fact that he is black than his politics. It was sickening, unfair and bias to the highest degree how different the interviews went!

When McCain was on there was hatred in their eyes. They did not even try to hide their hate for him! Barbara Walters who should be the one professional amongst the group just glared him down. She looked at him as if she would rather hit him in the face than talk with him! Then you had Whoopee Goldberg who rolled her eyes continually and made remarks about being made a slave again if McCain got in. As if she knows the first thing about slavery or does any other black person for that matter!

If you dared to criticize the women at the "VIEW" about their rude behavior they would probably say that "if you can't stand the heat then get out of the kitchen." Obviously meaning that as a presidential candidate McCain should be able to deal with it. But, why should McCain have to deal with the heat (which he does quite well at!) when Barack is in the kitchen they would lovingly bake him an apple pie and hand feed it to him!

The "VIEW" episode is just one example of the extreme hatred I have seen among liberals. The celebrities are the worst. It seems like almost every celebrity is flat out pissed off that McCain and Palin even exist. Now let's talk about Sara Palin; before she came on the scene the democrats thought they had the presidency in the bag! Then out of know where this young, beautiful, down to earth Hockey mom comes from Alaska. To add insult to injury she is younger than Obama, intelligent and far more appealing to the eye! She was also the most popular governor in the entire country with approval ratings of 80% or better! She was also tough and it is said that Alaska was strewn with the bodies of her victims. Not innocent victims but corrupt politicians who were abusing Alaska. She cleaned them up out of righteousness and a sincere desire to make her state better for the people. She has sincere intentions and people know it. She is just your average American woman with a desire to make the world a better place and did not get into politics for personal motives. She may not have been the most well-read candidate and I don't necessarily think she had the qualifications to be VP, but I certainly don't think Obama is any more qualified to be president.

At first the liberals were in shock and disbelief! Soon that shock turned to anger and they started attacking her along with McCain. They did not need to know who she was. Just the fact that she was a white republican and affiliated with McCain was enough! The liberal attacks on her and her family were just plain mean. All of the standard dysfunctional Hollywood fuck ups jumped on the bandwagon to thrash her. Like P Ditty who I have already mentioned ranting and raving on his video blog wondering who and where this Bi@#h

Palin came from? Then threatened that they would not let her take this election from Obama! Whatever that means? Then of course you have the standards like good old lesbo Rosie O Donald putting her down, then Matt Damon, the sl@t Pamela Anderson and scores of others.

There is one thing aside from being celebrities that most of these people have in common. They are immoral, partiers, arrogant, sexually dysfunctional (meaning they are either gay, bi or cheat on their spouses or are sexually promiscuous); they have drug and alcohol addictions, they are materialistic (things are their god), many are atheists, they have relationship problems and they live in a fantasy world of over indulgence. Again this is a generalization and I don't mean they are all that way. However, anyone who would listen to the opinions of some of the most dysfunctional and ungrounded people in the world would have to be a few bricks shy of a full load themselves. These celebrities are so far removed from the real world that it isn't funny! How celebrities that make ridiculous sums of money for a ridiculously small amount of work and live their lives in mansions, on the cover of magazines and are worshiped like gods could have an inkling of an idea of what Main Street American goes through is beyond me? Some may have come from Main Street, but they no longer live there.

I mean do they really think that if everyone were like them the world would be a better place? Should we all be sexually immoral, materialistic, atheistic, drug addicts? That is what they are teaching our children to be. They need to make movies and stop pretending that they know anything else! Their influence is only negative!

I am very surprised that someone like Obama would even be considered as a candidate for the presidency in the first place? He was at the time a first term senator and had been campaigning for the presidency two of those years; I mean out of all the experienced and knowledgeable people in The U.S. to choose from, why Obama? The Presidency of the United States is the highest office in the world and carries with it the most responsibility! Why would anyone consider a first term senator with very little experience? He should still be in his apprenticeship program not running for president! This has nothing to do with racism; it has to do with experience!

The president should be experienced in every area of politics and world affairs and preferably have executive experience, military experience and a strong love of country and an un-selfish desire to make the world a better place! Not just because he is a cool black guy. But, that is precisely why many people are voting for Obama, because they think he is a smooth talking, cool black guy! As I mentioned before a lot of young people are for Obama without knowing the issues. They just want to see a cool black guy as president and don't have the maturity to understand that the fate of the world could be at risk as a result of their choice.

When many people look at McCain they see an old fart, and his 30+ years of experience in politics just say to them that he is stagnate and an out of date old fart. They don't see experience, they just see out of date. When his POW experience is brought up, some will say. "Yes he was a hero once upon a time, but that does not mean that I have to vote for him." Not fully comprehending exactly the sacrifices he made for this country. No selfish person would have had the courage to endure what McCain did.

Remember the North Vietnamese were going to release him much earlier if he just agreed to make a few dishonorable statements regarding the U.S. to benefit North Vietnamese propaganda. But instead he stayed true to his country and instead of being released to go home and enjoy the freedoms of America that most of us take for granted he stayed for 5-1/2 long years being badly tortured in a small 4'X 6' cell. Most Americans now days can't go a day without their morning latte and have road rage at the most minor of travel inconveniences. Most of us are spoiled and out of touch with true sacrifice. We just want our stuff and our creature comforts. How many of us really have a clue like McCain does?

No one could say in all honesty that this is a selfish man with selfish interests! No way! He may be old and broken, but he has wisdom and strength beyond nearly all of us. He may not be tall, cool, handsome and young or black, but he knows the true meaning of sacrifice and has the strength and experience everyone should want in a president!

I thought it was offensive when the Obama campaign released a clip about how out of date McCain was and made it sound like he was too stupid and out of date to even send a basic email; when in fact he was so physically broken when fighting for America that the pain interferes with his ability to do so. That shows unbelievable disrespect on Obama's part. It's kind of like how teenagers treat their parents, like we are the idiots! McCain does not walk with a loose cocky swagger like Obama, but remember Obama has not had all of his fingers and arms and legs broken as a POW like McCain has.

Now I can't expect everyone who wants to be president to have experienced the hardships McCain has but, McCain just happens to be a unique man in history who has had an enormous amount of international experience, political experience and one who has seen a great deal of world history; in addition to his unique experiences as a POW that most presidents will never face. So, the way I see it we were very lucky to have a presidential nominee with the vast experience that McCain has! It would be foolish for the American people not to choose a president with the overwhelming knowledge that McCain has combined with his love of country and will to sacrifice himself for the nation's best interest! Unfortunately the nation was too out of touch to realize this and handed the presidency to Obama whose theories come from studying history in books, but McCain has the rare value of touching, feeling, smelling, hearing, tasting and experiencing history first hand!

Well maybe I am just a racist? That is how many would see my views. However, if there were black men like Colin Powel running for president I would vote for someone like that! If there was a black woman running for president like Condoleezza Rice I would seriously consider voting for her. What's the difference? Not skin color that's for sure, but experience, selfless service and proven abilities. I would vote for a black man, because skin color is not the issue. Character and experience is the real issue. I use the word arrogance, because you would have to be arrogant or ignorant to think that you could be a good president with hardly any experience. Obama came from nowhere with no experience and was treated like a rock star. It is ridiculous! It almost seems like he is a professional actor that has been groomed to play the part of a president! There is no history to show that he has the credentials to be the president and his popularity shows just how superficial many Americas are!

He debates well and speaks well, but has no hands on knowledge of the things he talks about. He hasn't been in the military, so he has no idea of what a soldier experiences, especially a soldier who has seen combat. I don't necessarily blame him for this, because even if he did serve in the military he might not have had any real combat experience. This lack of experience makes him even further removed from the experiences that John McCain went through and again this is no discredit to Obama, because few people, who have a combination of political experience, also have military experience and the experience of being a POW. This is just a rare combination that is hard to beat and Obama can't even come close. I really think there should be a checklist to qualify before you can even run for president.

I did believe P Ditty's threat that if McCain and Palin won the white house, the liberals would not have accepted it graciously. They would have held violent protests and people would have been hurt. When Obama won the Republicans were disappointed, but there was no mass protesting and complaining that the liberals would have done. Violence seems to be a liberal thing. It's funny that liberals protest the war and capital punishment, but they themselves are some of the most hostile and violent people in America. Liberals hate rules and if they ran this country without the balance of conservatives there would be total anarchy.

Some of the things I have in common with liberals and some of the things I don't are as follows:

They are usually pro- environment, as am I. The difference is the extremity of their beliefs. Some feel that humans should have absolutely no impact on it, where I believe it should be preserved, but also enjoyed; even including such controversial recreational activities such as the use of ATVs. There should be some ATV parks set aside for recreation because fun is good for the soul! Other areas should be left to hiking only.

I believe in responsible logging, like select cutting and replanting. However, I also believe that some forests should never be touched, like the ancient old grown forests and parts of the rain forests. They should be left to grow and evolve as nature intended. Another problem that liberals create with their no touch policy is that if you restrict land owners ability to profit from their land somewhat the result can end up much worse. An example might be a protest in logging on a piece of land. If the owner can do nothing with their land then they might resort to selling it to a developer or someone else who will exploit it? In my opinion it would be better to let them harvest, but in a responsible manner and to replant. This is better than losing the forest forever as can be the un-intended result of liberal protests.

Many liberals are also animal activists. I agree with preserve of nature and all species of animals, but I don't disagree with some hunting as they do.

Hunting can eliminate negative effects that come from the over population of certain animals.

Crime and punishment; Liberals don't believe in capital punishment, because they don't want to hurt anybody. However, the net result of not having strict policies is more death and in crueler forms, because evil people will continue to murder, torture, rob and rape unless the penalties are harsh, and although criminals enjoy destroying innocent lives by way of the cruelest methods imaginable they themselves do not want to be hurt or to suffer. Unfortunately, by good intentions you can create even worse problems than you hoped to solve. That is because of the evil nature of some people. Many of which I personally don't believe can be re-habilitated.

Liberals are light on crime and the net result is criminals running rampant. Look at the Somalia pirates for example who attacked 64 ships in one year. Many countries don't have the backbone to just stop it! They pay huge ransoms to these criminals! I think it is ridiculous that this is allowed to continue, but liberal politicians are too soft to act. Sometimes you have to fight fire with fire; otherwise countries will continue to be intimidated by a handful of primitive pirates. Arm and train all crewmembers that pass through these waters and give them the authority to destroy pirates. In addition war ships with the authority to destroy pirates should patrol these waters! I can almost guarantee that the visits by these criminals will go way down, but if you keep giving in to them then it will continue. This is liberal insanity! Efforts are finally being taken in earnest to solve this problem by force which has made a huge impact over the last few years, because force is the only way to deal with this threat.

Liberals are pro-alternative lifestyles. They think that homosexuality should be welcomed and embraced. They don't see any problem with men marrying men and women marrying women. They think you should be able to do whatever you want. Now, I will not claim that I know whether homosexuality is biologically predetermined or not? However, I do believe that in many cases it is a perverted choice by dysfunctional people without values, morals or religion. It is a fact that men and women were designed to be with each other sexually. Otherwise procreation would be impossible.

A man and women's genitals are designed to work together for the purpose of procreation; an anus is designed for bowel movements. OK, this should all be pretty simple stuff! And to use parts for something other than what they are intended for has proven to be hazardous to a person's health. I.E. AIDS. I am not saying people should not have the right to be sexually perverted as long as it does not involve children and both parties are consensual. However, the negative side effects from this open policy are the children who learn from example.

If some people are predetermined to be homosexuals, others may not be, but follow that path as a learned behavior from the same sex parents whether it is in their household or from television. This really skews nature as it was intended. I am not far right on this, but I think that the way the liberals push it so hard into the public is un-healthy and confusing for our children and results in homosexuals that are not biologically predetermined to be homosexual, plus it promotes perversion and an anything goes mentality. The Rossi O Donald's and Ellen DeGeneres who are always in the spotlight can make things very confusing to kids and should not go out of their way to promote their lifestyle. At the same time I certainly do not agree with those who violently target homosexuals. Live and let live, but don't go out of your way to corrupt society for the sake of those not afflicted with your illness!

Liberals don't really like authority having its hand on every aspect of our daily lives, but if we did not have some more conservative views for a balance we would live in a very strange and violent world. The perfect world of their fantasies could not exist.

Chapter 21

Germans and their Nazi past

I have always been morbidly fascinated with World War 2, especially with the Nazis. Although, I enjoyed watching movies and documentaries on the war with Japan as well, it never fascinated me like the war in Europe? I don't really know why, but I think it is because I am an American of Northern European ancestry and the Germans seemed so similar, but yet, so different? The Nazis were such dark and sinister characters in my mind. As a child growing up in America you could always find World War 2 movies on T.V. and plenty of documentaries. Later in my adult life came the History channel, which regularly airs documentaries and offers historical perspectives on World War 2 and the Nazis. I certainly did not idolize the Nazis. My feelings were quite the contrary I thought what they did was horrible! But I became curious about how such horrible things could have ever happened on such a large scale? These things were happening in cities that resembled the U.S. The people looked the same, dressed the same and had the same religion as us. If the people in Germany resembled us so closely (at least outwardly) could that sort of thing happen here?

As a child growing up every American kid I knew was familiar with the history of World War 2 and the Nazis. We would dress up in our army clothes and go outside and play war games all day long. The bad guys were always the Germans or the Japs. Germans were portrayed as evil and the Americans were always the good guys, so the Germans had to die in the end. All we really knew was that the Germans were bad and hated Jews. At the time I really never knew what a Jew was or why they were hated? Some of the World War 2 movies would show the Germans treating the Jews horribly! To me as a child I did not understand why this was?

I knew what prejudice was, because of the prejudice between whites and blacks in America. However, there is a significant difference in the way whites and blacks look and act, but I could not see the difference between Jews and Germans? They both looked white to me. How could you even know who a Jew was? When they were dragging Jews to concentration camps, it just looked like they were dragging white Europeans to the concentration camps. Jews usually had dark hair, but so did many Germans. It made me wonder if I might be a Jew. Although, I had blonde hair and blue eyes I might still be a Jew, because some Jews had blonde hair and blue eyes too.

I really did not know anything about religion at the time, although we occasionally went to church. I did know that Christ was a Jew and that Germans were Christians who prayed to Christ, so this made it all the more confusing to me as an eight year old boy! One movie I watched showed some German kids picking on a boy and calling him a Jew. They made fun of his big ears and his big nose. Having once myself been teased about my ears I began to think that I might be a Jew? But why were they so hated? Certainly not because of their superficial characteristics alone! I mean they were really hated! They were murdered by the millions, forced into slavery, starved to death and tortured! Another thing that confused me was that there was not a Jewish army provoking war against Germany. All the battles were between the Americans and other Europeans. The Jews were just like innocent civilians on the sidelines who did nothing wrong. I could not figure the whole thing out. I really did not know why there was a World War 1 and a World War 2?

Later in life these questions intrigued me to research the subject as a hobby. I read every book I could find on World War 1 and 2, watched every documentary and even learned to speak, read and write in German, so I could understand Hitler's speeches and read Nazi propaganda. I read Mein Kampf to try to understand the man. Why was this monster at one time the most popular statesman who ever lived? Why did the people love him so, and in the end follow him to destruction?

When you watch Eva Braun's (Hitler's mistress) home movies, Hitler looks like a decent loving man. These home movies were silent, but now computer technology has advanced to the point where we can now read the lips (even from a side angle) and have the conversations translated to see what all the participants in the videos said and even how they sounded. A rare recording of Hitler's voice recorded by the Finnish military in 1941 was recently found where he is speaking in a normal tone. They have used this to simulate what the normal everyday casual conversations must have sounded like?

They found the conversations to be nothing out of the ordinary. They were simply the pleasant conversations you would hear at any barbecue among friends. Hitler was pleasant to his guests and seemed to genuinely love animals and children! Some videos did show his animosity towards Herman Goring and a few others, but overall they were civil.

I was simply fascinated with the whole era. I tried to visualize what it must have been like to be in Europe during World War 2. In America we have never been subject to our cities and towns being carpet-bombed or soldiers fighting in our streets. We have never had families torn from their comfortable homes and life's and thrown into concentration camps then put to death in gas chambers. These people were not criminals! They were women, children and old men.

It all seemed so horrific and surreal! The thing that really made it all so interesting is that Germany was an open, civilized, cultured nation like anywhere in Northern and Western Europe or America. How could such a civilized, educated, cultured nation systematically murder millions of people? Especially the Jews who did not even have an army fighting against them.

I wanted to understand. The Germans are so similar to us. In fact the largest ethnic group in the United States is of German ancestry.

Why did this happen? It is such a sad story for everyone! Are the Germans really evil by nature? Obviously they can't be! So, why did the overwhelming majority enthusiastically follow Hitler?

In order to understand why this happened one needs to look much deeper into German history than just the history of World War 2. In fact you really need to start at the beginning of German history to understand some of it. Since this is not a history book I will not delve into Germany's entire history, but I will touch on some key events that lead to the Nazi era.

Germany was not a country per say before 1871, but rather a patchwork of German speaking principalities. World War 1 was in part the result of the assassination of Archduke Franz Ferdinand and his pregnant wife Sophie by a 19-year-old Serbian by the name of Gavrillo Princip from Sarajevo. The Austrian Empire wanted Serbia to allow the Austrian police force access to Serbia, so they could interrogate and apprehend the perpetrators and bring back the Serbian assassin(s) for trial. The refusal of the Serbs to allow this resulted in the German- Austrian-Hungarian and Ottoman Empirical (Central Powers) army(s) marching into Serbia to retrieve the culprit(s) and as a result of that the countries allied with Serbia (Triple Entente Powers) took up arms and this escalated into war.

In my opinion it would have been a much simpler fix to let the Serbian assassin be tried and executed for murder rather than have years of war and millions of lives lost! It really makes me question the logic of the human race! To think that the release of one assassin to the Central Powers may have prevented the loss of approximately 70 million lives between the two wars. After all he did assassinate an Archduke, his wife and their unborn child. The Austrian-Germanic request did not seem unreasonable. So, did the Germans really carry the entire responsibility for the war(s) as many would like to believe?

When the Germans lost World War One the victorious nations wanted revenge for the four years of suffering and split Germany into pieces, dividing it among the conquering nations leaving native Germans behind newly formed borders, isolated from their country and under foreign rule. The Germans were also required to pay reparations to the victorious nations. The price they had to pay to the victors was so exorbitant that it bankrupted the nation. The humiliated and bankrupt country was barely surviving and could not afford to keep paying these huge reparations. In addition the overwhelming majority of the Germans did not understand why in the final end they lost World War 1. They saw only their military victories. They felt that the politicians and the Jews of the provisional Weimar Republic had sold them out by agreeing to the Treaty of Versailles. Jews of course were well rooted in German politics and society. To many they were viewed as a parasite without a country of their own and who sucked the lifeblood out of other nations by involving themselves in the politics and the finances of other nations. These were some of the reasons the Jews were hated, but also they were hated because of their religion. They were responsible for the death of Jesus Christ and the majority of Europe was Christian. The Germans believed that the Treaty of Versailles was a peace conference and not surrender. The Germans grew suspicious of the communists and the Jews who they saw as benefiting from the treaty and who had supposed extra national loyalties. The Bavarian Soviet Republic who ruled Munich for two weeks in 1919 made up mostly of Jews and communists helped fuel the propaganda, which lead to the concomitant rise of Nazism.

Because of the Treaty of Versailles and the part the supposed non-nationalistic Jews and communists of the Weimar Republic played. The message that Hitler preached was just what the conservative nationalistic Germans wanted to hear. Hitler convinced the already anti-Semitic ethnic Germans that they needed to unite and rid the country of this cancer that was destroying their beloved Vaterland.

Almost every country involved thought the penalty imposed on Germany was too harsh with the exceptions of the French. Field Marshal Ferdinand Foch said this is not a Treaty, but rather a 20-year armistice, which would result in another war. 20 years and 65 days later his predictions were proven correct!

After years of studying the history of the two World Wars I at least had some understanding of how this all could have happened. I could actually understand the German frustration and at the same time feverishly disagree with how it was handled!

The Germans were forced into a corner and they had to fight or die. Fighting for survival can bring out tremendous a rage in a person or in a prideful nation and morals often become secondary at this point.

When I look at this part of history and see how before September 1939 Hitler had regained all of Germanys previously lost territory, I can't help, but wonder why he didn't stop there. It seems logical to be satisfied with regaining the territory and restoring the economy and national pride. Germany had also already stopped paying reparations and was becoming prosperous again. Although much of the prosperity was from building up a war machine, which would have been necessary to complete these goals, it still seemed like there were options to avoid war. He already proved he could accomplish great things without firing a shot by regaining the territory.

I can also understand the Germans suspicion of Jews, foreigners and communists. I can also understand the desire to preserve the German race as well. However, I cannot understand wanting to wipe out a race of people. I can understand the dislike of the Jews and communists, but he could have deported them and or created the nation of Jerusalem like the U.S. Helped establish in 1948. That way they would be out of your hair and no longer influencing your nation, politics, economics or ethnic makeup. He certainly had the power to do that and would have gone down in history as a great man had he chosen that route. Unfortunately the hate ran too deep to do the logical thing!

The horrors committed by the Nazis were inexcusable, but at the same time you can't blame the average German citizen. Even though the majority followed the Nazis you need to understand where they came from and how they became desperate enough to do so. Plus remember in the beginning Hitler was seen as a savior and not a villain. Adolf Hitler offered and provided jobs and restored a sense of national pride, strength and unity, he regained the territory lost in the Treaty of Versailles without firing a shot. For a people demoralized and disgraced he was a savior! He gave the ethnic Germanic people value and confidence in themselves and convinced them that the communists, Jews and others stabbed them in the back. If they could cleanse Germany of the enemy they could restore and maintain Germany's greatness! The average German did not know the horrors that would follow.

The allied nations had a great deal of responsibility for the outbreak of the two world wars. Not releasing that single individual to the German-Austro-

Hungarian Empires or allowing them to search for the culprit(s) was a big mistake! The Serbs hated the German and Austro-Hungarian Empires and by not handing over an assassin to them for trial was an act of rebellion. The French also hated the Germans and it was this hate that started World War 1 which led to World War 2. So it is not just the Germans who harbored animosity and hatred. There were also other factors involved like the arms race, nationalism, imperialism, militarism and the alliance system. However, it was the assassination and the lack of cooperation by the Serbs that ignited the flame!

It was the English that invented the concentration camps during the Boer wars in South Africa in the late 19th century, not the Germans. The Americans used flamethrowers to burn the Japanese soldiers alive in their foxholes and caves and who carpet-bombed civilian targets in both Europe and Japan. The Americans also dropped the atomic bombs on Hiroshima and Nagasaki killing approximately 220,000 civilians with two planes and two bombs. However, the English and Americans won the wars they fought, so the atrocities they committed are justified in their minds. But what if the Germans had won? Then they would have painted a picture of inhumane brutality on the part of the defeated nations. They would be the heroic victors who vanquished the world from evil! At least this would be the view of those with a voice. All those who disagreed or were destroyed would not have a voice and the history books would paint a different picture! I am not trying to say that Germans or any combination of countries are good or that the Americans or any combination of countries are bad. However, I am saying that it is all- subjective and all nations are capable of unspeakable evil when they feel justified!

The Allied nations thought it was necessary to win the war regardless of how many innocent people were lost. Does this make them sadistic or evil? Although, no one knows the true mind of Hitler, perhaps he also firmly believed that killing innocent civilians was a necessary evil. Maybe in his mind he did not want an endless war of eternal suffering? He may have truly wanted peace at the end of it all, but thought war was the only way to achieve peace in the end? He might not have been as sadistic as many believed? Maybe he just thought, as did the allies that he needed to destroy the evil so the good could survive and flourish? Remember that the English first bombed Berlin before the Germans started bombing London in retaliation. These are details that are seldom mentioned.

Hitler once made a peace offering to England and wanted the war to end. However, Winston Churchill rejected it and vowed to fight on until the already conquered countries were free. In the beginning Hitler did not want war with England, nor probably even France for that matter? However, once Poland was invaded France and England declared war on Germany. Although, Hitler should not have invaded any country, he felt that his goals were justified in order to benefit his people, just as the Americans thought they were justified in killing American Indians and stealing their land. The Germans are extremely vilified, but the heroic allies were also guilty of crimes against humanity and extreme hatred and racism. We are all aware of this, but it is mostly overlooked because in the end, it is the winner who is righteous and who writes the history books.

The Germans had a problem with foreigners in the first half of the 20th century and still do. Even today some complain of the rising crime rate, which is mostly committed by foreigners. Even though now they have to handle the situation more carefully do to political correctness, the UN and because of their past treatment of the Jews. However, most European countries are having similar problems with immigrants. It has been statistically proven that immigrants from certain nations are responsible for the rising crime rate. So why deal with them so delicately? Political correctness is why. In Hitler's day he was not restricted by political correctness and used an iron fist to deal with the situation.

You just can't do those things now days! Of course you should not be able to treat human beings the way the Nazis did either. However, by going to the opposite extreme we are endangering our nations. Can't there be someplace in the middle? Firm, but fair! Hitler had a vision of an idealistic world and the evils that he felt were necessary were only temporary until his ideal world could be created. He had no concern for anyone other than the Germanic people, but you have to have a concern for other races and cultures, because we all share this earth together and you can't just take out the people you don't like! But, that does not mean we should allow immigrants to migrate to our countries and commit crimes or upset the social fabric of our nations.

Germany and other nations have gone from an iron fist policy to a kid glove policy and neither one is correct. Restrictions need to be firmer. It is not fair for nations to put up with crime and a flood of immigrants because of how politically correct they are expected to be. A nation should be able to protect itself.

It is kind of like de-segregation in the 1960's. Both whites and blacks were forced to go to school together. However, you shouldn't be forced to send your children to a particular school, but you should also not forbid a child to go to a school in their district or of their choosing. Even today in America segregation is happening all over again, but this is the choice of the parents. Parents are conscientious of the crime rates in certain areas and schools, and any parent who loves their child will not send them to a crime ridden school just to be politically correct, just as a nation should not have to grant citizenship to immigrants from countries notorious for crime. A mixture of races in schools has overall been a good thing in American and in some areas and schools a blend of students has been a positive step. But there are other areas that are crime infested and no loving parent is going to put their child into a dangerous situation. Of course these crime-infested areas should not be abandoned or ignored either. There should be efforts to re-educate and police these crime infested schools and neighborhoods.

I am amazed at how certain areas are notorious for gangs and crime, yet the problem persists. In areas like these an iron fist might be the only thing that works? Mussolini and Hitler caused a lot of terror, but at the same time they did away with a majority of the violent crime. In Italy the Mafia was imprisoned. It was only when the Americans and British took control of the country that they unwittingly released these criminals back onto the streets.

A strict policy works for Singapore and at the same time the citizens are happy and feel safe, proving that you don't have to be a Mussolini to enforce the law. The over whelming majority of the people have no desire to break laws anyway, because they know that they are designed to protect the people and improve the quality of life for everybody. Therefore, they have no fear of the strict penalties.

There are many misdemeanors that are committed every day in the US, but the penalties and chance of getting caught are small enough to where people don't worry about it, moreover the people that commit these infractions just don't seem to care!

I was leaving Lake Washington after a day of boating with friends and family and noticed an obese black woman in a huge SUV with spinners twirling, stereo blasting and the base thumping. At the same time this woman was hurling out profanities at passing cars and throwing her empty 32-ounce drink out of the window as well as a bag of McDonald's garbage. She did this very casually as if this was normal. For her and many Americans just like her, I have no doubt that it is normal! Is this their way of enjoying the freedoms and liberties of the U.S.? Why do these types of people want to live in filth? Why do they want things to be ugly? Do they think that things are ugly anyway, so what difference does it make? I know some countries are very clean, because I've seen them, so why is it so bad in the US?

I think some of it has to do with the racial and cultural makeup of the United States and also that the laws are way too soft. If people had some pride in their environment there wouldn't have to be strict laws, but many people have no pride in themselves, let alone their environment. The US is the wealthiest and most powerful nation on Earth, yet many of its citizens are some of the fattest, laziest, immoral, spoiled and vulgar slobs around. No wonder the French hate us! It probably hasn't helped the relationship between the two countries much when big, fat, loud and obnoxious Americans go on holiday in France and are rude and demanding!

Then on top of it all they brag about how they won the war for them and say things like "if it hadn't been for the US you French would be speaking German right now!" The French must be in disbelief when looking down at a table of rude, fat Americans throwing out insults like this knowing full well that these particular Americans couldn't even climb out of a fox hole, let alone save France from the Germans. Many brave American men died, so that many other Americans could have the freedom to become fat, lazy and rude! What a shame! All of this wealth and victory has in many cases brought over indulgence and lethargy. Far too many of the tourists from America do not look like the victors that helped liberate France in the 1940's, nor do they act like them! If you're proud to be an American, then be courteous and show some kindness and respect. Represent your nation in good character and set a good example. No matter what country you're visiting, being rude and offensive is never OK and is an embarrassment to the nation you represent! Even if the French are rude to you, don't react in kind. It might take them a while to get use to the new Americans?

I know it sounds like I am really thrashing the Americans, but keep in mind that I am only thrashing some of them. I admire a lot of things about my country and the people who live here. The U.S. is still the best country on earth. However, there is a downward spiral among many Americans which affects the country as a whole and it is not just a few bad apples, but a major tide of bad behavior. If this is not kept in check then the bad behavior could become the majority and bring down this great nation by the sheer weight of numbers.

On one hand we have some of the best athletes in the world. This was proven at the 2008 Beijing Olympics with the U.S. winning more metals than any other nation, but at the same time our cities are ripe with crime and poverty. We have the most powerful military in the world, but can't manage to secure our own borders. We have some of the most intelligent and educated people in the world too, but also have a 60% drop out rate among Hispanics and inner city African Americans. We have one of the most beautiful natural environments in the world with 2000 year old redwood forests, rain forests, deserts, snowcapped mountain ranges, and beautiful ocean beaches, but many treat these areas with no respect by polluting our waters, littering, and excessive logging and over development. We have some of the nicest people in the world and also some of the vilest! We have freedom of speech, but many don't really understand what the intent for that was and many use this right for no practical purpose at all other than to display how foal they can be! To me this is an abuse of our freedoms and liberties! We have the right to bear arms, but we suffer approximately 10,000 gun related deaths each year. What I am really saying is that we have it all! But, we are choking on our liberties and could lose it all as a result!

NEW POLICIES

Below are some general ideas for a set of new policies that I think we should consider in the United States and other countries to improve our nations and the world:

Illegal immigration and border control:

Make the penalties well known to foreigners and build a defense against illegal entry. A first offense is a warning and education phase on how to obtain legal citizenship and the penalties for violations, then deportation. A second border offense is critical and will result in permanent deportation with no chance of obtaining citizenship. A third offense will result in imprisonment.

Fourteenth Amendment

Section 1.

"All persons born or naturalized in the United States, and subject to the jurisdiction thereof, are citizens of the United States and of the State wherein they reside".

I realize that arguing the 14th Amendment is treading on thin ice. However, this clause makes little sense to me! How can the child become a citizen and not the parent, since parents are a necessity to the child? Therefore, my belief is that children born on US soil and having illegal parents will NOT automatically become U.S. citizens and will be deported along with their parents to their country of origin. The U.S. should no longer tolerate the Anchor Baby Mentality! Most other nations do not allow this, so why should we?

Cultural and racial identity:

A balance of races and cultures should be preserved. Couples procreating within their own race should be entitled to tax benefits. Couples with rare or endangered features or recessive genes such as red or blonde hair, blue or green eyes should get tax benefits for procreating with-in their race. Rare Native American populations, authentic Hawaiian races or any other rare or vulnerable ethnicity should also be entitled to tax benefits for the preservation of their ethnic makeup. The goal is to keep vulnerable races and traits from disappearing in this racially mixed up society in which we live.

Gun control and gangs:

All gang's should be disbanded and members will be disarmed, weapons destroyed and ALL gun sales should be illegal without obtaining all documentation from consumers and preforming a thorough background check in addition to reporting all records to government authorities for review and approval before firearms can be purchased.

Gangs should be outlawed as well as gang logos, colors, rituals and tattoos.

All gang members should be required to complete a life course. The course should include: Life management skills, finances, job training, succeeding in school, health, birth control and even an etiquette course. Financial aid should be available for secondary education with special rates and conditions for the rehabilitation of gang members.

Welfare policy

All welfare recipients should be required to be on birth control and also should be required to attend a family planning course and job-training program. Recipients will be required to participate in a community service activity at least one day a week and attend a class one day per week.

Welfare will be limited. Habitual repeaters receiving benefits should have no more than 2 children. If they already have more than 2 children they should be required to stay on birth control for the remainder of their child bearing years. The second cycle of welfare should be partially repaid by community service or monthly installments to deter abuse of the benefits paid for by the taxpayers. Appeals can be made and granted for special circumstances.

Crime

Child molesters should suffer the same consequences as those accused of murder. The exception should only be in the event of two teenagers engaging in sexual activity. An example would be a 13 to 15 year old engaging in consensual sexual activity with a 16 to 21 year old. This will be considered statutory rape and should be penalized as such. This should no longer be tolerated and violators should no longer get away with a slap on the wrist and registered as a sex offender.

The death penalty should be used only in cases where the murder is in the first degree and guilt has been proven beyond a doubt. The most heinous murderers such as serial killers should be put to death within 30 days from the time guilt is proven beyond a doubt.

The Economy

The U.S. should remain a free enterprise system. However, the U.S. government should regulate huge corporations with the potential to disrupt the overall economy, as was the example of Bear Stearns, Lehman Brothers, Merrill Lynch, AIG, etc.

The Federal National Mortgage Associations of Freddie Mac and Fannie Mae should have the former regulations before MBS unregulated private label securitization conduits became common practice.

Federal bailouts should not and will not be part of a free enterprise system.

The society as a whole should not have to pay for the irresponsible actions and greed of a few. In the future and if for some reason regulation fails the U.S. government will not bail out any company that engaged in risky business practices. Furthermore, if their business practices affect the overall economy in the way it did during the great depression in 1929 and in 2008 all of the Proprietors, Presidents, Vice presidents, CEOs and others involved in the day-to-day decision making should be subject to a criminal investigation. No more golden parachutes for the few while the masses suffer. This selfish mentality should not go un- punished.

Monopolies should not be allowed. The free enterprise system needs competition for the benefit of the consumer.

National Security

A reasonable and up to date military should remain in place for the defense of the U.S. The military is primarily for the defense of the U.S. and should not be expected to police the world. In some situations it will be necessary to intervene in other countries to maintain our security at home as well as the security of our allies.

Rough nations like Rwanda, Somalia and Uganda, which have suffered horrific human right violations, may be offered help in the event that they follow international rules even if they are not a member. All nations should be required to follow the rules laid out by an international body such as NATO or separate entity. All international members will agree to carry an equal proportion of the responsibility according to their resources and population.

Human rights violations should not be tolerated and those governments, warlords or mercenaries who disrupt the nations people, as is the example of some of the above mention nations should be subject to the forfeiture of their sovereign nation and should in effect be govern by an international body. If you can't maintain the peace and safety of the people's with-in your own nation then an international body will have to do it for you. All people deserve peace and security wherever they live!

Piracy will be eliminated by any means. An international ship that is being attacked by pirates will have the right and responsibility of defending themselves by any means. An international body should share the responsibility of policing international or national waters and should have the authorization to destroy any pirate or pirate vessel. International security should have the authorization to enter national waters or land to apprehend and destroy pirates. There should be no safe haven. The complete destruction of pirates will serve as a deterrent to future acts of piracy; meaning that the goal is not for the apprehension of pirates, but for the destruction of pirates. Governments should not waste taxpayers money apprehending, imprisoning and bringing pirates to trial. If some think this is too severe of a policy then the solution is simple; don't engage in piracy!

International Governing

Nations will need to be governed to maintain balance with-in a country. This means that if a nation has a population of 10 million people, but only has the resources to maintain a good quality of life for 7 million, then the birth rate must be adjusted to reach the goal of 7 million. This is not a fascist ideology here! Everyone has the right to life and the right to bear children. This policy will only help to determine how many children at a given time. If the population dips below a certain percentage then women can have more children.

If the population rises then women will have to have less children. However, regardless of the situation all women will be entitled to bear at least one or two children. This goal may take generations to reach, but in time and without human rights violations, the people will reach a balance, and through a continuation of this policy future generations will enjoy the benefits of enough food to eat, education, jobs, peace and a healthy and safe environment with plentiful renewable resources.

Is it more humane to watch people suffer and starve or to engage in family planning? This is a sticky issue because it might seem like a form of fascism. However, here is how I see it: If we continue to allow the population to grow un-bridled, then we will destroy our environment or eventually the population will correct itself by way of starvation, war and disease. Things might even get so bad that governments allow populations to die out by not providing basic services like medical, food, shelter or police service in high risk areas. If times get desperate enough then euthanasia might be implemented for the elderly, sickly, handicapped and criminals. With limited resources there may be no other choice?

In my proposal of balancing the population by way of family planning, and balancing populations based on resources, what is the most suffering that would occur? Well, maybe you would only be able to have two children and not ten? Prospective parents should also be required to be licensed to meet the minimum requirements to have children. No one wants to be told how many kids they can have, but the alternative of starvation, war, increased crime and disease, depletion of natural resources, or all out anarchy seems a whole lot worse to me!

Not only will we need to balance populations, but also we will need to get to a point where we use re-usable energy and discontinue the use of fossil fuels and stop deforestation. An international body will need to be involved in implementing and enforcing anti-deforestation policies like in the South American rain forest. Although these are sovereign nations the forests that grow on them impact the entire world, and with that at stake it is essential that forestry practices be monitored and regulated in all nations.

Greed

As of the date of this writing the world economy is in great peril because of the irresponsibility of a few on Wall Street. It is not only ridiculous, but should be a crime for so many to have to suffer because of the extreme over indulgence of a few. I certainly don't believe in communism where everyone is equally poor. However, the excesses in capitalist societies are ridiculous and dangerous. How much money does one person need anyway? This is no longer about becoming successful and providing a good life for your family and self. Greed is one of the most dangerous diseases that there is. It is one of the 7 sins and it not only destroys the greedy, but it trickles down to destroy the common people who just want to live a decent life.

It is nice to have some extras if you want to put in the extra work to obtain them. If someone works very hard then there should be no saying that they can't buy a nice home on the lake, a boat, nice cars and take a ski vacation to the Swiss Alps in the winter and then another vacation to Tahiti in the summer or wherever? To me this would be a very good life! However, the greed on Wall Street, organized crime and in politics goes way beyond this.

It becomes a sickness and there are overly indulgent people who pay exorbitant prices for things they do not need or probably really even want, but they buy these superfluous things merely as a means to flaunt their status. They pay for these excesses simply because they can. They also do it because they are braggadocios. It is a symbol of their power and wealth more than anything practical. Money comes before anything to many, including god, family, friends or health. If money is their god then their god is fleeting as was displayed during the great depression and which reared its ugly head again in 2008.

It is these few greedy people who are responsible for most of the planets destruction. There are examples of rich celebrities taking champagne baths in Crystal or Dom Perignon while they wear million dollar blood diamonds, just because they can. Poachers murder the Giant Gorillas in Africa just so they can cut off their hands and sell them to the rich for souvenir ashtrays. To me this is beyond belief!! What a wasteful, cruel and unworthy goal. The rich look down on the poor as if they are an unworthy class of people. They toy with the waiter or waitress at a fancy restaurant constantly complaining about any minor inconvenience. Even if the waiter or waitress was perfect they will find something to complain about just for an excuse to belittle someone. This also apparently gives them a sense of power. They purchase via the black market and horde valuable stolen artifacts which are a link to our ancient past just so they can display them in their own private collections and use them as a bragging tool for the few guests who will ever see them, when they should be in a museum for the world to understand, study and enjoy.

The greedy are the real unworthy class of people. I am not saying all of the rich, but the greedy! You can be well off and still put god, family and the good of society first. But when money and power comes before all, then that is truly unworthy.

In October 2008 congress passed a 700 billion dollar bill for a Wall Street bailout, despite the out pouring protests from the public to their congressmen and women, here is how it should have worked:

Allow the banks to fail and establish new banks in their place with the regulations needed. The owners, presidents and CEO's who profited at the expense of the world should go home with nothing! No golden parachutes at all. Moreover, they should be investigated for illegal activity and prosecuted. If the corporate lawyers find that they have broken no laws, which will undoubtedly apply, in the above case since we know whom they work for. Then make new laws to make this risky speculation illegal!

The new owners, Presidents and CEOs will have pay caps. This sounds like socialism, but I don't see a problem with the government having tighter regulations for banks when it affects the world economy in such a negative way. At least there will be regulations and security. As we are a government for the people, the banks are also for the people and not for the bankers. Our money should not be their piggy bank to gamble with.

A portion of the bailout should have gone to the homeowners, or the loans should have been restructured into fixed rate mortgages with rates between 3.0 to 4.0%. The government has tried these stimulus packages before. However, giving a person $600.00 is a joke. If you gave each homeowner $100,000 in this situation we would see a major change in the economy given the present situation! The rules for the cash would be that it goes towards the mortgage of your home only! Many people would be able to pay off their entire mortgage and others would pay off enough to make their payments affordable. The banks would have a combination new money coming into the banks, which they could in turn re-lend, and a major number of re-finances to re-structure the homeowner's payment. In most cases this would be enough to keep people in their homes and eliminate most foreclosures solving the housing crisis.

Let's say to use simple math that there is 300 million people in the U.S. Divide this by four estimating a family of four. This gives us 750,000 families. Multiply this by 64% of those families as homeowners or 480,000 homeowners. Then multiply this by $100,000 to each homeowner. That gives us only 48 billion dollars of the proposed 700 billion dollar bail out. This leaves 652 billion to restructure banks, increase the FDIC limit, etc. This would be very popular with the people because the government would be working from the bottom up! Plus the difference it would make would be something every American could see! 700 billion going to Wall Street would, and has been invisible to the average person. Of course this would seem unfair to future homeowners who don't get $100,000 towards their house, but this would be a one-time deal to eliminate the problem with the sub-prime loans. There is some fairness to this though in the respect that every homeowner would benefit and not just the people who dug a hole for him or her by getting into a sub-prime mortgage. A homeowner with a low interest rate with a fixed rate loan would also benefit. An added benefit to the responsible people out there would be that if you have been paying on a home for years and owed less than $100,000, the remainder could be kept by the individual for any other reason. I.e. Retirement, college, home improvement or whatever else and pumped back into the economy!

Another even less drastic solution could have prevented years of suffering, by simply relieving every home owner of their sub-prime interest only, adjustable rate mortgage and implementing a flat revised 3% fixed rate mortgage. If this had happened, I bet most people would have been able to keep those homes which now set vacant and rotting!

REFERENCE LIST

Martin Luther King Jr. quotes www.abcnews.com *Pg.5*

Civil War statistics www.history.com; en.wikipedia.org/American_civil_war Pg.12. Chapter 1 "What is a Racist?"

www.ourdocuments.gov *Pg.13 "Fort Laramie Treaty"*

www.drivebyplanet.com Pg.16 "Eva Herman"

Bing images "Somalia Pic" Pg.17

Pg.18.Bing images "Lucerne Pic"

www.newsbbc.co.uk/2/hi/europe/3113430stm Pg. 19> Christoph Blocher

Fox News February 2008: Bill 'O Reilly's interview with Geraldo Rivera on illegal immigration. Pg.23. Chapter 3 Deportation

Author: Geraldo Rivera. Pg.24 "His/Panic". Chapter 3 Deportation

www.stormfront.org Pg.25; Chapter 3 Deportation Illegals bankrupting hospitals on the U.S. Mexico border.

Bing Images "Swedish Girls Pic" Pg.41. Chapter 5: Blonde Haired, Blue-eyed Extinction.

LA County demographics; www.Davikservices.com; October 22, 2006 San Diego Union Times article by Douglas Belkin/2002 Loyola University Chicago; study conducted by Mark Grant. Pg.37-42. Chapter 4: Extremes vs. Balance

www.jewishvirtuallbrary.org; www.en.wiki.pedia.org; www.pbs.org; www.spiegel.de/demography; "Blondes to die out in 200 years" BBC News, September 27, 2002. Pg.44. Chapter 6 "Lebensborn"

9 billion in population by 2050 www.news.bbc.co.uk Pg.56. Chapter 9 "Blame Game"

www.economist.com/node/15959332 Pg.57. Chapter 10 "Population Control"

www.deutschwelle.de Pg.62, Chapter 12 "Crime" Angela Merkel;

ABC News; www.abcnews.go.com/20/20 Pg.68. "Happiness" Chapter 13

www.deutschwelle.de Pg.78. Immigration/crime

www.forbes.com/billionairs; www.census.gov/huffington; Huffington Post. Pg.84. Chapter 16 "Greed"

www.history.com/topics/wwii Pg. 105. "Germans and their Nazi Past" Chapter 21

Printed in Great Britain
by Amazon.co.uk, Ltd.,
Marston Gate.